V.I. LENIN

IMPERIALISM
THE HIGHEST STAGE OF CAPITALISM

ISBN: 978-1-63923-559-9

Printed: January 2023

Published and Distributed By:
Lushena Books
607 Country Club Drive, Unit E
Bensenville, IL 60106
www.lushenabks.com

ISBN: 978-1-63923-559-9

CONTENTS

V.I. Lenin

INTRODUCTION

By Doug Lorimer

I. LENIN'S AIMS IN WRITING THIS WORK

The term "imperialism" came into common usage in England in the 1890s as a development of the older term "empire" by the advocates of a major effort to extend the British Empire in opposition to the policy of concentrating on national economic development, the supporters of which the advocates of imperialism dismissed as "Little Englanders". The term was rapidly taken into other languages to describe the contest between rival European states to secure colonies and spheres of influence in Africa and Asia, a contest that dominated international politics from the mid-1880s to 1914, and caused this period to be named the "age of imperialism".

The first systematic critique of imperialism was made by the English bourgeois social-reformist economist John Atkinson Hobson (1858-1940) in his 1902 book *Imperialism: A Study*, which, as Lenin observes at the beginning of his own book on the subject, "gives a very good and comprehensive description of the principal specific economic and political features of imperialism" (see below, p. 33).

Lenin had long been familiar with Hobson's book. Indeed, in a letter written from Geneva to his mother in St. Petersburg on August 29, 1904, Lenin stated that he had just "received Hobson's book on imperialism and have begun translating it" into Russian.[1]

In a number of his writings between 1895 and 1913, Lenin had noted some of the characteristics of the imperialist epoch, for example: the concentration of production and the growth of monopolistic trusts and cartels, the growing importance of the export of capital compared with the export of commodities, the internationalisation of capitalist economic relations, the struggle between the rival European powers to partition the world market, the parasitism and decay of capitalism, and the creation

---

Doug Lorimer is a member of the National Executive of the Democratic Socialist Party.

through capitalism's socialisation of production of the material conditions for the transition to socialism.

However, it was not until the outbreak of the World War I in August 1914 that Lenin felt the need to make a comprehensive and systematic *Marxist* analysis of the nature of the imperialist stage of capitalism, i.e., to go beyond the analysis made by Hobson in 1902 and by the Austrian Marxist economist Rudolf Hilferding in his 1910 book *Finance Capital*. The latter work, Lenin stated in his *Imperialism: The Highest Stage of Capitalism*, "gives a very valuable theoretical analysis of 'the latest phase of capitalist development', as the subtitle runs" (see below, p. 33)[2].

Given his comments on both Hobson's and Hilferding's works, why then did Lenin feel the need to produce his *own* analysis of imperialism? Lenin himself provides the answer in his 1920 preface to the French and German editions of his book. The "main purpose of the book", Lenin explained, was "to present, on the basis of the summarised returns of irrefutable bourgeois statistics, and the admissions of bourgeois scholars of all countries, a *composite picture* of the world capitalist system in its international relationships at the beginning of the 20th century — on the eve of the first world imperialist war". In doing this, Lenin had three objectives in mind:

1. To prove that "the war of 1914-18 was imperialist (this is, an annexationist, predatory war of plunder) on the part of both sides" and thus to refute the arguments of the leaders of the Second International, above all those of its leading theorist, Karl Kautsky, that each side in the war was merely fighting for "national defence" and therefore there was nothing opportunist or class-collaborationist in these leaders supporting the war efforts of the governments of their own countries.

2. To counter the theoretical arguments of Kautsky about the nature of imperialism and to demonstrate that he was "obscuring the profundity of the contradictions of imperialism and the inevitable revolutionary crisis to which it gives rise".

Kautsky did this, firstly, by arguing that it was wrong to "identify with imperialism all the phenomena of present-day capitalism — cartels, protection, the domination of the financiers, and colonial policy". That is, according to Kautsky, imperialism was not a "phase" of capitalist economic development but a "special policy" of capital, which "consists in the striving of every industrial capitalist nation to bring under its control or to annex ever bigger areas of *agrarian* territory, irrespective of what nations inhabit them".[3] Secondly, proceeding from this view of imperialism, Kautsky argued that this "special policy" might be superseded after the world war by a new policy, that of "the *extension of the policy of the cartels to foreign policy, the phase of ultraimperialism*", i.e., the peaceful uniting of all the rival finance groups into a single, world-wide trust and the "abolition of imperialism through a holy alliance of the imperialists".[4] Lenin sought to counter this argument by demonstrating that imperialism was the *highest and last stage* of the development of capitalism. 3. To demonstrate that there was a causal connection between this new stage in the development of capitalism and the existence of a relatively stable opportunist, pro-imperialist, trend within the working-class movement of the "advanced" capitalist countries. As Lenin noted at the end of his 1920 preface:

> Unless the economic roots of this phenomenon are understood and its political and social significance is appreciated, not a step can be taken toward the solution of the practical problems of the Communist movement and of the impending social revolution.

However, the "economic roots of this phenomenon" and its "political and social significance" were only outlined briefly in the book. They were taken up more thoroughly in the article "Imperialism and the Split in Socialism", printed here as an appendix. This was published in *Sbornik Sotsial-Demokrata* — the war-time theoretical supplement to *Sotsial-Demokrata*, central organ of the Russian Social-Democratic Labour Party (Bolsheviks) — in October 1916, a few months after Lenin had completed writing his book on imperialism. The book itself was written between January and June of 1916, though Lenin started research for it in mid-1915. However, it was not published until the middle of 1917.

II. THE FUNDAMENTAL CHARACTERISTICS OF THE NEW STAGE OF CAPITALISM

The closing years of the 19th century and the opening years of the 20th had been marked by a succession of wars — between China and Japan in 1894, Spain and the USA in 1898, Britain and the Boer republic in South Africa in 1899, Japan and Russia in 1904, Italy and Turkey in 1911, the Balkan states and Turkey in 1912, and between the Balkan states themselves in 1913. This ascending wave of wars culminated in outbreak of the first world war in 1914.

The "Great War" of 1914-18 brought into stark view a significant quality that had marked, on a growing scale, the wars of the "age of imperialism" — the struggle between the "Great Powers" for hegemony of the world and the control of its economic resources, actual and potential. It constituted concrete evidence that, as Lenin put it in his 1920 preface to his *Imperialism*:

> Capitalism has grown into a world system of colonial oppression and financial strangulation of the overwhelming majority of the people of the world by a handful of "advanced" countries. And this "booty" is shared between two or three powerful

world plunderers armed to the teeth (America, Great Britain, Japan), who are drawing the whole world into *their* war over the division of *their* booty.

Imperialism was therefore not to be explained as merely a change in the *foreign policies* of the governments of the "advanced" countries, but as a change in the nature of *capitalist relations of production*. While cautioning that it was necessary not to forget "the conditional and relative value of all definitions in general, which can never embrace all the concatenations of a phenomenon in its full development", Lenin pointed out that if it were necessary to "give the briefest possible definition of imperialism we should have to say that imperialism is the monopoly stage of capitalism". Such a definition, he added, "would include what is most important, for, on the one hand, finance capital is the bank capital [i.e., the money capital] of a few big monopolist banks, merged with the capital of the monopolist associations of industrialists; and, on the other hand, the division of the world is the transition from a colonial policy which has extended without hindrance to territories unseized by any capitalist power, to a colonial policy of monopolist possession of the territory of the world, which has been completely divided up".

Lenin noted "five basic features" as the imperialist stage of capitalism:

> (1) the concentration of production and capital has developed to such a high stage that it has created monopolies which play a decisive role in economic life; (2) the merging of bank capital with industrial capital, and the creation on the basis of this "finance capital", of a financial oligarchy; (3) the export of capital as distinguished from the export of commodities acquires exceptional importance; (4) the formation of international monopolist capitalist associations which share the world among themselves; and (5) the territorial division of the whole world among the biggest capitalist powers is completed.

Taken separately each of these phenomena shows a *degree* of becoming a difference in *kind*. But in their totality, they represent a *transformation of quantity into quality* — a qualitatively new stage in the development of capitalism. Taken as a whole, their central characteristic is the transformation of free competition into its opposite, into *monopoly*. This indicates that the distinguishing features of imperialism are not to be dismissed as superficial or temporary aberrations, accidentally modifying the "normal course" of capitalism. They indicate that the *essential* production relations of capitalism have developed *all* the potentialities latent within their primary antagonism (socialisation of the productive process and private appropriation of the results of this process), and that before any further development of the social relations of production is possible the antagonism itself must be eliminated. This can be seen most clearly if we examine in succession each of the five basic features of imperialism distinguished by Lenin.

III. MONOPOLY AS THE LOGICAL OUTCOME OF CAPITALISM

The concentration of capital and of production in the hands of fewer and fewer firms follows inevitably from the social conditions of capitalist production, among which the most general are (a) the social division of labour from which springs the differentiation of the various branches of production, and (b) private ownership of the means of production. Given these things and competition exists in its germinal form. Given the further development of (a) commodity production and (b) the appearance on the market of *labour-power* as a commodity, and the conditions exist for the development of competition into its capitalist form. Capitalist production bursts the bounds which constrained competition and made it an essential and a universal condition of production. Competition imposed upon each capitalist owner of means of production the need to cheapen the production of commodities. In other words, it made it imperative for each capitalist firm to produce on a *higher* scale, i.e., with larger masses of better organised and more thoroughly exploited workers equipped with more mechanised instruments of production. In short, capitalism both extended and intensified competition, and with it the elimination of the less well-equipped producers. The logical end of this elimination could be none other than one solitary ultimate victor.

Concretely, however, certain difficulties must be overcome before this end can be attained. The field of direct competition is divided into different branches of production and a number of different centres (local and national markets which only in their aggregation constitute a world market). Thus before a lone survivor could be reached on a world scale, lone survivors must first have been evolved in each of these branches of production and in each of these centres.

But the evolution of an absolute monopoly in any one branch of production (steel production, say) on a world scale cuts across and conflicts with the evolution of a monopolist control of any local or national market, or economy. Thus the tendency towards monopoly, the more sure and certain it becomes, cannot realise itself in a smooth, linear fashion but must proceed *dialectically*, i.e., by the creation and progressive surmounting of a whole series of violent antagonisms. Moreover, since the rate of development, owing to physical, historical and political conditions, as well as economic ones, cannot help but vary from time to time, from industry to industry, and from country to country, the force and complexity of these antagonisms and their dialectical consequences cannot help but be multiplied beyond all reckoning. Hence, although the tendency towards monopoly must be recognised as an absolute law of capitalist production, it by no means gives grounds for the utopian reformist-socialist dream of a peaceful transition, through a regular process of "inevitable gradualness", from capitalist competition to a world monopoly (or a number of national monopolies) which could be peacefully "taken over" by the state "on behalf of the people".

If the process is viewed not in its abstract *unity*, but in its concrete and multiform *totality*, it will be seen that the tendency toward monopoly is one that can only realise itself *approximately*, and never *absolutely*, since in its concrete forms each detail tendency engenders a resistance to itself which can only be transcended by engendering resistance on a higher plane, and so on, progressively, until a crisis either of war or of social revolution (or of both) is precipitated.

In other words, while the tendency towards monopoly does in fact involve the negation of competition within a number of spheres of production and exchange of commodities, it produces at the same time over the whole field of capitalist economy, and still more over the whole field of bourgeois society, an intensification of competitive antagonisms, so that the (approximate) attainment of monopoly, instead of eliminating competition (and antagonism) from society, on the contrary, *raises them progressively to a higher and more destructive scale*. This is seen most clearly when it is borne in mind that competition is of many kinds. There is, for example, the general competition between those who buy and those who sell, as well as the competition of the sellers and buyers among themselves. The elimination of competition among the sellers, instead of eliminating competition among the buyers, only intensifies these latter forms of competition.

The tendency towards monopoly is concretised into a system with the emergence of a new category of capital, that of *finance capital*. This again gives an example of the transformation of quantity into quality. As a capitalist industrial enterprise (in steel production, for example) rises to a position of monopolistic dominance in its specific industry it finds itself, as trade fluctuates, at one time possessed of more money capital (realised profits) than it needs for the expansion of its business and, at another, faced with emergency needs for fresh money-capital. In the one phase it invests its surplus in bank capital; in the other it gives a share in its capital to the bank in exchange for a loan. A parallel process goes on with the banks, and the two complementary processes end with the merging of the capital of a monopolistic industrial firm and a monopolistic banking company to form a new type of monopolistic enterprise which transcends the limitations of industry and banking each in themselves, and carries the process of *domination* to a higher and a more comprehensive scale. With the formation of finance capital begins the process of bringing the economy of the country of its origin under the domination of a small group of financial oligarchs.

This process has another and even more far-reaching aspect. Insofar as monopoly is attained it makes possible (if only temporarily) the stabilisation of prices and the limitation of production to the estimated needs of the monopoly-controlled market. By doing this, relative excess of production is eliminated along with redundant managerial and sales staffs. As a result, the monopoly obtains an increased volume of profit in circumstances which preclude further investment of capital within its own sphere. Hence the export of capital takes on an ever-growing importance. The world becomes partitioned more and more, and in two distinct ways. Economically, the export of capital facilitates the development both of horizontal and of vertical monopolies, i.e., the bringing of a given industry under the control of an *international* monopoly, and the establishment of monopoly control of a *series of industries* which work up raw material from its point of natural origin to its final complete form. These processes intersect, collide, and also combine to give rise to higher forms of monopoly. Ultimately, both of them converge on the two extreme points of (a) control of the sources of origin of indispensable materials and (b) control of markets in which to dispose of finished products. Both thus add impetus to the partitioning of much of the Earth's territory into "spheres of influence" among the rival imperialist powers. And since this process of imperialist partitioning had been completed (approximately) by the end of the 19th century — and the economic forces impelling imperialist expansion still continued — it followed of necessity that there had to become manifest yet another transformation of "quantity into quality": the process of imperialist expansion brought the imperialist powers (the politico-military representatives of rival financial oligarchies) to the point at which further expansion could only be attained at each other's expense.

The history of monopoly capitalism is at the same time the history of the strengthening of the state power within each of the "advanced" capitalist countries and its use to further the interests of the finance capitalists of its own country on the world market. At the beginning of this process the spokespeople of the most advanced and most expansionist capitalist powers were often quite forthright about the use of state power to defend and promote these interests. Thus, in 1907, Woodrow Wilson, who was to become US president in 1912, declared: "Concessions obtained by financiers must be safeguarded by ministers of state, even if the sovereignty of unwilling nations be outraged in the process."[5] Wilson's secretary of state William Jennings Bryan was equally candid, telling a gathering of US financiers: "I can say, not merely in courtesy — but as a fact — my department is your department; the ambassadors, the ministers, and the consuls are all yours. It is their business to look after your interests and to guard your rights."[6]

By the beginning of the 20th century the penetrating power of finance capital had brought about a complete transformation of the relations between the "sovereign states" which made up what bourgeois journalists and bourgeois politicians loved to call the "community of nations". Whereas in diplomatic theory all sovereign states meet and do business as equals (i.e., equally "sovereign" within their territory), finance capital brings into being a differentiation of states into debtors and creditors. This inter-linking of states, the subordination of the great majority of states to the financial overlordship of a few financially rich powers, supplements the open territorial partition of the world. Its result was that by 1914 virtually every state in the world outside the few "Great Powers" (Britain, France, Germany, Japan, the USA and Russia) was a financial vassal of one or another of these "empires". And, since each of these "empires" was impelled by the need to "expand" still further, it could only expand at the expense of one or more of the others. Thus the cause of imperialism (and imperialist war) was shown to be the development of capitalism into a new and higher stage in which its antagonisms had reached a point that further development could only be expressed through veiled or open inter-imperialist war on the one hand, and in potential or actual revolutionary uprisings on the other.

Summing up this whole process, Lenin wrote in December 1915:

> It is highly important to have in mind that this change was caused by nothing but the direct development, growth, continuation of the deep-seated and fundamental tendencies of capitalism and production of commodities in general. The growth of commodity exchange, the growth of large-scale production are fundamental tendencies observable for centuries throughout the whole world. At a certain stage in the development of exchange, at a certain stage in the growth of large-scale production, namely, at the stage that was reached approximately at the end of the nineteenth and the beginning of the twentieth centuries, commodity exchange had created such an internationalisation of economic relations, and such an internationalisation of capital, accompanied by such a vast increase in large-scale production, that free competition began to be replaced by monopoly. The prevailing types were no longer enterprises freely competing inside the country and through intercourse between countries, but monopoly alliances of entrepreneurs, trusts. The typical ruler of the world became finance capital, a power that is peculiarly mobile and flexible, peculiarly intertwined at home and internationally, peculiarly devoid of individuality and divorced from the immediate processes of

production, peculiarly easy to concentrate, a power that has already made peculiarly large strides on the road to concentration, so that literally several hundred billionaires and millionaires hold in their hands the fate of the whole world.[7]

IV. THE HIGHEST AND LAST STAGE OF CAPITALISM

It may be objected that, while Lenin showed that imperialism was a new and higher stage of development of capitalism, he did not and could not show that this was the "highest" possible developmental stage of capitalism. The answer to that objection is that it proceeds from the assumption that the possibilities of development open to a given historically-conditioned social form of production are unlimited. The whole facts and processes analysed by Marx, and Lenin, show on the contrary that only a specifically limited and conditioned development of the productive forces is possible to each historically determined social form of production:

At a certain stage of their development, the material productive forces of society come in conflict with the existing relations of production, or — what is but a legal expression for the same thing — with the property relations within which they have been at work hitherto. From forms of development of the productive forces these relations turn into their fetters. Then begins an epoch of social revolution.[8]

Two outstanding phenomena indicated by Marx as characteristic of the culminating phase of capitalism are shown by Lenin to have developed in the monopoly finance stage. These were (1) parasitism and (2) the partial recognition of the social character of production. The formation of joint-stock companies involves, Marx observed:

1. Tremendous expansion in the scale of production, and enterprises which would be impossible for individual capitals. At the same time, enterprises that were previously government ones become social.

2. Capital, which is inherently based on a social mode of production and presupposes a social concentration of means of production and labour-power, now receives the form of social capital (capital of directly associated individuals) in contrast to private capital, its enterprises appear as social enterprises as opposed to private ones. This is the abolition of capital as private property within the confines of the capitalist mode of production itself.

3. Transformation of the actual functioning capitalist into a mere manager, in charge of other people's money, and of the capital owner into a mere owner, a mere money capitalist. Even if the dividends that they draw include both interest and profit of enterprise, i.e., the total profit (for the manager's salary is or should be simply the wage for a certain kind of skilled labour, its price is regulated in the labour market like that

of any other labour), this total profit is still drawn in the form of interest, i.e., as a mere reward for capital ownership, which is now as completely separated from its function in the actual production process as this function, in the person of the manager, is from capital ownership. Profit thus appears (and no longer just the part of it, interest, that obtains its justification from the profit of the borrower) as simply the appropriation of other people's surplus labour, arising from the transformation of means of production into capital, i.e., their estrangement vis-a-vis the actual producer; from their opposition, as the property of another, vis-a-vis all individuals really active in production from the manager down to the lowest day-labourer. In joint-stock companies, the function is separated from capital ownership, so labour is also completely separated from ownership of the means of production and of surplus labour. The result of capitalist production in its highest development is a necessary point of transition towards the transformation of capital [as means of production — DL] back into the property of the producers, though no longer as the private property of individual producers, but rather as their property as associated producers, as directly social property. It is furthermore a point of transition towards the transformation of all functions formerly bound up with capital ownership in the reproduction process into simple functions of the associated producers, into social functions ...

This is the abolition of the capitalist mode of production within the capitalist mode of production itself, and hence a self-abolishing contradiction, which presents itself *prima facie* as a mere point of transition to a new form of production. It presents itself as such a contradiction even in appearance. It gives rise to monopoly in certain spheres and hence provokes state intervention. It reproduces a new financial aristocracy, a new kind of parasite in the guise of company promoters, speculators and merely nominal directors; an entire system of swindling and cheating with respect to the promotion of companies, issues of shares and share dealings. It is private production unchecked by private ownership.[9]

In a supplementary note to the first edition of Volume 3 of Marx's *Capital*, Engels wrote in 1894 that "since 1865", when Marx wrote the above quoted comments, "a change has occurred that gives the stock exchange of today a significantly increased role, and a constantly growing one at that, which, as it develops further, has the tendency to concentrate the whole of production, industrial as well as agricultural, together with the whole of commerce — means of communication as well as the exchange function — in the hands of stock-exchange speculators, so that the stock exchange becomes the most pre-eminent representative of capitalist production as such". Engels explained that in 1865:

... the stock exchange was still a *secondary* element in the capitalist system ... Now it is different ... accumulation [of capital] has proceeded at an ever growing pace, and in such a way moreover that no industrial country ... can the extension of production keep step with that of accumulation, or the accumulation of the individual capitalist be fully employed in the expansion of his own business ... With this accumulation, there is also a growth in the number of rentiers, people who have tired of routine exertion in business and who simply want to amuse themselves or pursue only a light occupation as directors of companies.[10]

Lenin did not have to invent a new theory to arrive at the conclusion that monopoly finance capitalism was the highest stage of development of capitalism. He merely had to show that the features that Marx had described as characteristic of this stage — joint-stock companies; separation of capital ownership from managerial functions in the immediate process of production; monopolies; the emergence of a "financial aristocracy"; parasitism in the form of rentiers, of nominal company directors and stock-exchange swindlers — had become the dominant and typical form of capitalist business activity at the beginning of the 20th century. Lenin's description of the monopoly finance stage of capitalism as its *highest stage* — the stage which exhausts its possibilities of "evolutionary" as distinct from revolutionary development — was a faithful application of Marx's conception of "capitalist production in its highest development", i.e., that the complete *socialisation* of the labour process involved the complete *separation* of the *productive function* of capital from the ownership of capital, a separation which becomes obvious when, in its parasitic rentier form, profit presents itself "as simply the appropriation of other people's labour" as a result of the alienation of ownership of capital from all individuals actually involved in the labour process.

This alienation is involved in capitalist production from the beginning. It is the inner relation which constitutes the essence of the capitalist form of commodity production. When, therefore, from being the inner relation connecting individual workers and individual capitalists in the production process, it becomes outwardly expressed as a fully-developed social antagonism — as a social conflict between the actual producers, *associated* by the production process into a collective individuality on one side, and the exploiting non-producers, equally associated by their ownership into a collective individuality *opposite* to theirs — it is obvious that (a) no further development of capitalist relations of production is possible; (b) that the social antagonism has become the starting point for a transition to a new social form of the productive process; and (c) that this starting point has its material basis and its general form in the positive and negative poles of the social antagonism itself, i.e., in associated production by associated owners for the satisfaction of their individual and common needs.

This was what Lenin meant when he described monopoly finance capitalism as "moribund", "decaying" capitalism — not, as is often assumed by his critics, that he was claiming it had become an *absolute* barrier to the revolutionising of the technical basis of production or to the quantitative expansion of productive forces. Rather, he argued that it had become a *fetter*, a constraint, on the fullest possible development of the productive forces, that it exhibited a *tendency* toward increasingly uneven development of the productive forces, and toward the stagnation of the growth of productive forces in the countries richest in capital:

> ... monopoly under capitalism can never completely, and for a very long period of time, eliminate competition in the world market (and this, by the by, is one of the reasons why the theory of ultra-imperialism is so absurd) ... the possibility of reducing the cost of production and increasing profits by introducing technical improvements operates in the direction of change. But the *tendency* to stagnation and decay, which is characteristic of monopoly, continues to operate, and in some branches of industry, in some countries, for certain periods of time, it gains the upper hand ...
>
> It would be a mistake to believe that this tendency to decay precludes the rapid growth of capitalism. It does not. In the epoch of imperialism, certain branches of industry, certain strata of the bourgeoisie and certain countries betray, to a greater or lesser degree, now one and now another of these tendencies. On the whole, capitalism is growing more rapidly than before; but this growth is not only becoming more and more uneven in general, its unevenness also manifests itself, in particular, in the decay of the countries richest in capital (Britain).[11]

Insofar as he treated the monopoly finance stage of capitalism as its highest stage, and, *therefore*, as the stage of capitalism that had created the material basis for the transition to socialism, Lenin was merely reiterating and reinforcing the conclusions already drawn, in germinal form, by Marx.

V. IMPERIALISM AND THE SOCIAL ROOTS OF LABOUR OPPORTUNISM

Lenin's description of monopoly finance capitalism as "dying" capitalism, as capitalism "in transition to socialism", also did not mean that he believed that this meant capitalism would *automatically* give way to socialism — as the reformist-socialists, beginning with Eduard Bernstein in the 1890s, argued, completely misrepresenting Marx's concept of the "inevitable collapse" of capitalism.

The beginning of an epoch of social revolution meant for Marx that further development of the productive forces made it *necessary* to *overthrow* the existing social form of production and replace it with a new social form. But if such a social revolution was not actually carried out, this would not mean that the existing social form would persist forever. To the contrary, once it had developed "all the productive forces for which there is room in it", this social form *would* collapse ("perish")[12], leading to a regression in the social form of production, to "the common ruin of the contending classes" — unless there was a "revolutionary re-constitution of society at large"[13].

If analysing imperialism as the culmination of the development of capitalism involved the application of Marx's theory of the concentration of capital (and production), so the extension and deepening by Lenin of Marx's conception of an epoch of social revolution as an epoch of the *decay* and *revolutionary overthrow* of capitalism (as distinct from and opposed to opportunist-idealist theories of its gradual "evolution" into socialism) involved an extension and deepening of Marx and Engels' analysis of the impact of monopoly under capitalism on the working class and what this entailed for organising a proletarian revolution.

Marx and Engels had frequently derided the English working class for becoming "more and more bourgeois" in its outlook during the period of the second half of the 19th century. England's working class at that time was the largest and by far the most organised in the world. Marx and Engels had observed, at close quarters, the growing efforts of the English labour leaders to win "respectability" with the employers and bourgeois politicians. Engels took up this issue in detail in his 1892 preface to the English edition of *The Condition of the Working Class in England*. He began by noting that England had developed into an exceptional capitalist country between 1848 and the 1870s. It held vast colonial possessions and enjoyed a virtual monopoly of industrial production within the world market. The English capitalists reaped immense profits from this monopoly, which they used a part of to grant important economic, cultural and political concessions to the English working class in exchange for its expected loyalty to the international policies of the English industrialists, a loyalty that was mediated and obscured through the fostering of "national pride" and English national chauvinism.

Engels concluded that the condition of the English working class had generally improved during this period, but that the concessions were unevenly distributed and primarily accrued to a "small, privileged, 'protected' minority [who] permanently benefited".[14] Even for the great bulk of workers, "There was temporary improvement

But this improvement always was reduced to the old level by the influx of the great body of the unemployed reserve, by the constant superseding of hands by new machinery, by the immigration of the agricultural population ..."[15]

Who, then, constituted the "privileged" and "protected" minority that was able, by and large, to stay out of the "reserve army" of unemployed and to avoid the full brunt of the "normal" mechanisms of capitalist production that undermined gains by workers? Engels identified two sections of the English working class — the factory hands (primarily located in the textile mills and iron foundries of the north) and the members of the "great Trades Unions" (headquartered in London). This minority of workers, he wrote, "form an aristocracy among the working class; they have succeeded in enforcing for themselves a relatively comfortable position, and they accept it as final ... They are model working men ... and they are very nice people indeed nowadays to deal with, for any sensible capitalist in particular and the whole capitalist class in general".[16]

Politically, Engels observed that it was prudent policy for the English industrial capitalists to form alliances with the better situated and organised strata of the rapidly growing proletariat. Perhaps the most striking change was in the industrialists' attitude to the labour unions. "Trades Unions", Engels wrote, "hitherto considered inventions of the devil himself, were now petted and patronised as perfectly legitimate institutions, as useful means of spreading sound economical doctrines amongst the workers. Even strikes, than which nothing had been more notorious up to 1848, were now gradually found out to be occasionally very useful, especially when provoked by the masters themselves, at their own time".[17]

The defeat of the Chartist movement in 1848, followed by a long period of concessions, had the "natural" corrupting result that the politically active sections of the working class, located entirely in the unions, began supporting England's colonial policy and adopting liberal-bourgeois politics as their own. Further, within the working-class movement, the more protected workers upheld exclusionary policies, particularly aggravating the split between English- and Irish-born sections of the proletariat.

From Marx and Engels' descriptions and analysis of the rise in England of labour opportunism — the sacrificing of the long-term interests of the working class as a whole to gaining immediate advantages for a minority of workers — Lenin abstracted out the central theoretical point: the stubborn phenomenon of opportunism among English workers had an *economic basis* in the fact that the dominant world position of English capitalism had produced *superprofits* which allowed the English bourgeoisie to make significant economic, cultural and political concessions to the "upper strata" of the proletariat. These concessions, a complex set of phenomena including expansion of the social wage, and access to educational, cultural and political institutions, denied to the lower mass of the proletariat, served as a material basis for the creation of a thoroughly opportunist, class-collaborationist trend rooted in a large *labour aristocracy* of privileged and protected workers as well as the conspicuous rise of bourgeois-reformist illusions and national chauvinism among the politically active English workers.

Lenin, however, did not rest with extracting the essence of Marx and Engels' analysis of opportunism in the working-class movement in 19th century England. Rather he extended and deepened this analysis by applying it to the imperialist stage of capitalism. Essentially, he argued that the emergence of monopoly capitalism had produced in a handful of countries the extended, rather than temporary, basis for the extraction of superprofits by the dominant section of the ruling bourgeoisie, the financial oligarchy. On the other hand, to assure continued political stability bourgeois rule increasingly required that the sections of the working class that tended to spontaneously become politically active — the better educated, better organised workers — be ideologically tamed into a "loyal opposition". This would be accomplished through using part of the superprofits of monopoly finance capital to *bribe* these sections with economic, cultural and political concessions. This basic development, Lenin contended, would be a feature of the class structure (and impact accordingly on the dynamics of the class struggle) in *every imperialist country*.

The leaders of the opportunist trend within the working-class movement would therefore find a stable base for their *conscious* attempts to keep the class struggle within the bounds of bourgeois legality and bourgeois social-reformism. This form of "mature" opportunism — as distinct from the spontaneous reformism which can be expected in the initial stages of any worker's political development — would emerge on the very foundations of a developed trade-union consciousness and movement in imperialist countries (oftentimes replete with socialist rhetoric!), and would be a *permanent feature of imperialism*.

Consequently, the split between opportunist and revolutionary trends within the working class of the imperialist countries could not be expected to evaporate, leaving behind some mythical, homogeneous, revolutionary-inclined proletariat. Revolutionary strategy and tactics would therefore have to take this permanent split in the working class of the imperialist countries into account from the beginning. Lenin posed the issue bluntly in his October 1916 article "Imperialism and the Split in Socialism":

> ... unless a determined and relentless struggle is waged all along the line against [the opportunists'] parties — or groups, trends, etc., it is all the same — there can be no question of a struggle against imperialism, or for Marxism, or of a socialist labour movement.

Lenin did not confine himself, however, merely to general statements concerning the need to struggle against the opportunist trend within the working-class movement. He attempted to draw out the concrete historical trends that shape the contours of such a struggle and serve as the basis for the elaboration of revolutionary strategy and tactics in the "advanced" capitalist countries in the imperialist epoch.

VI. MARXIST TACTICS IN THE EPOCH OF IMPERIALISM

In his October 1916 article "Imperialism and the Split in for Socialism", Lenin noted (and contrasted) two opposing, but connected, historical tendencies at work in the development of the spontaneous working-class movement. On the one hand, workers, particularly the better-situated workers, organise in economic combinations (trade unions) to fight their employers for better wages and conditions, and to force the bourgeois state to recognise their economic gains through labour legislation. The better-situated workers, precisely because they are better-situated, tend to be the politically active section of the working class, the section out of which spontaneously emerges the advanced workers who are consciously drawn toward revolutionary socialist politics.

On the other hand, the very success of the economic and political struggles for reforms by the better-situated workers compels the bourgeoisie to seek new forms of maintaining its control over the better-situated workers. Meanwhile, the existence of monopoly superprofits and the fact that the workers' combinations can inevitably represent only particular sections of the working class lay the basis for the bourgeoisie to manipulate this contradiction and use concessions to bribe the better-situated workers and thus to foster among them the idea that they can achieve continual improvements in their position simply through struggles for reforms. In this manner, the gains of the better-situated workers can be turned into their opposite, serving not to strengthen the working-class movement as a whole but to provide a basis to split and weaken the movement through the victory of opportunism among the better-situated workers, and thus limit the number of advanced, revolutionary-minded workers who emerge from their ranks.

Lenin attached central importance to this dialectic, targeting in particular those who one-sidely argued that workers' combinations into trade unions would inevitably lead to ever higher forms of struggle and consciousness, while downplaying the ability of the bourgeoisie to utilise such combinations (among other factors) to forge a labour aristocracy on a profoundly opportunist basis.

Lenin argued that Marxist tactics required a sober view of the labour aristocracy, its hegemony in the mass organisations of the working-class movement, and the necessity to conduct a vigorous ideological struggle against the opportunist politics of the privileged strata within the working class by championing the interests of the lower, "unprotected", mass of the class. This understanding of the necessity to champion the interests of the non-aristocratic sections of the working class against the opportunist politics of the labour aristocracy did not mean that Lenin advocated that Marxists abandon political work among the better-situated workers. To the contrary, it was a call for Marxists to struggle against the opportunist politics of these workers. This struggle proceeds on two fronts: against the reactionary leaders of the labour aristocracy, against the "labour lieutenants of the capitalist class", whom it is necessary to expose and discredit as conscious agents of the bourgeoisie within the working-class movement, and to replace them with consciously revolutionary leaders; and to destroy the political influence of the labour aristocrats within the ranks of working-class movement, a portion of whom may be won away from opportunist politics in the course of the struggle.

Lenin's understanding of the material basis for the existence of a consolidated opportunist trend within the working-class movement provides a basic orientation for revolutionary Marxist politics in the imperialist countries. It is evident from Lenin's materialist analysis of this phenomenon that the strategic task of preparing the proletariat for socialist revolution in these countries is inconceivable without qualitatively weakening the political influence of the opportunist trend. However, consistent with the materialist method, Lenin's analysis reveals that this is not possible at all times, since the strength of opportunism is directly related to the strength of monopoly capitalism internationally and within any particular imperialist country.

Periods of relative imperialist prosperity will make the task of combating the political influence of opportunism within the working-class movement extremely difficult. However, revolutionary political work in these "slow" periods lays the basis for the quality of advances in periods when the objective conditions create possibilities to seriously contend with the opportunist trend.

Periods of economic and political crisis, which are inevitable, call for open and sharp struggle against opportunism, which becomes even more dangerous and virulent to the working-class movement when its material base is narrowed. The weakening of the material bribe of economic, cultural and political privileges to the better-situated workers in such periods increases the importance to the bourgeoisie of the ideological and political services of the opportunist "labour leaders". The loss of privileges or their threatened loss will not necessarily provoke a spontaneous abandonment of opportunism within the upper strata of the working class. On the contrary, it can fuel a powerful reaction within these sections to "blame" the workers in the lower strata or in other countries for the loss or threatened loss of these privileges. Nonetheless, the loss of the relative privileges created out of imperialist prosperity will steadily erode the social base for opportunism, thereby creating more favourable circumstances for workers to grasp the real role of the opportunist "labour leaders" and to better understand their own class interests.

Whether the full potential of the objective conditions will be realised or not depends on the political line, tactics and organisation of the revolutionary Marxists. This is precisely the significance of "Leninism", which opportunists of all hues never tire of dismissing as "voluntarism", completely inappropriate to the imperialist "democracies".

Finally, Lenin warned that Marxists should have no illusions about "quick results" in defeating the domination of the working-class movement in the imperialist countries by the opportunist trend, even in a period of deep social crisis. In these countries, he later wrote, "we see a far greater persistence of the opportunist leaders, of the upper crust of the working class, the labour aristocracy; they offer stronger resistance to the Communist movement. That is why we must be prepared to find it harder for the European and American workers' parties to get rid of this disease than was the case in our country".[18] +

Preface to the Russian Edition

THE PAMPHLET HERE PRESENTED to the reader was written in the spring of 1916, in Zurich. In the conditions in which I was obliged to work there I naturally suffered somewhat from a shortage of French and English literature and from a serious dearth of Russian literature. However, I made use of the principal English work on imperialism, the book by J. A. Hobson, with all the care that, in my opinion, that work deserves.

This pamphlet was written with an eye to the tsarist censorship. Hence, I was not only forced to confine myself strictly to an exclusively theoretical, specifically economic analysis of facts, but to formulate the few necessary observations on politics with extreme caution, by hints, in an allegorical language — in that accursed Aesopian language — to which tsarism compelled all revolutionaries to have recourse whenever they took up the pen to write a "legal" work.

It is painful, in these days of liberty, to reread the passages of the pamphlet, which have been distorted, cramped, compressed in an iron vice on account of the censor. That the period of imperialism is the eve of the socialist revolution; that social-chauvinism (socialism in words, chauvinism in deeds) is the utter betrayal of socialism, complete desertion to the side of the bourgeoisie, that this split in the working-class movement is bound up with the objective conditions of imperialism, etc. — on these matters I had to speak in a "slavish" tongue, and I must refer the reader who is interested in the subject to the articles I wrote abroad in 1914-17, a new edition of which is soon to appear. Special attention should be drawn to a passage on pages 119-20.* In order to show the reader, in a guise acceptable to the censors, how shamelessly untruthful the capitalists and the social-chauvinists who have deserted to their side (and whom Kautsky opposes so inconsistently) are on the question of annexations, in order to show how shamelessly they *screen* the annexations of *their* capitalists, I was forced to quote as an example — Japan! The careful reader will easily substitute Russia for Japan, and Finland, Poland, Courland, the Ukraine, Khiva, Bokhara, Estonia or other regions peopled by non-Great Russians, for Korea.

---

* See p. 118 of the present volume.

I trust that this pamphlet will help the reader to understand the fundamental economic question, that of the economic essence of imperialism, for unless this is studied, it will be impossible to understand and appraise modern war and modern politics.

Author
Petrograd April 26, 1917

Preface to the French and German Editions

I

As was indicated in the preface to the Russian edition, this pamphlet was written in 1916, with an eye to the tsarist censorship. I am unable to revise the whole text at the present time, nor, perhaps, would this be advisable, since the main purpose of the book was, and remains, to present, on the basis of the summarised returns of irrefutable bourgeois statistics, and the admissions of bourgeois scholars of all countries, a *composite picture* of the world capitalist system in its international relationships at the beginning of the 20th century — on the eve of the first world imperialist war.

To a certain extent it will even be useful for many Communists in advanced capitalist countries to convince themselves by the example of this pamphlet, *legal from the standpoint of the tsarist censor*, of the possibility and necessity, of making use of even the slight remnants of legality which still remain at the disposal of the Communists, say, in contemporary America or France, after the recent almost wholesale arrests of Communists, in order to explain the utter falsity of social-pacifist views and hopes for "world democracy." The most essential of what should be added to this censored pamphlet I shall try to present in this preface.

II

It is proved in the pamphlet that the war of 1914-18 was imperialist (that is, an annexationist, predatory, war of plunder) on the part of both sides; it was a war for the division of the world, for the partition and repartition of colonies, and spheres of influence of finance capital, etc.

Proof of what was the true social, or rather, the true class character of the war is naturally to be found, not in the diplomatic history of the war, but in an analysis of the *objective* position of the ruling *classes* in *all* the belligerent countries. In order to depict this objective position one must not take examples or isolated data (in view of the extreme complexity of the phenomena of social life it is always possible to select any number of examples or separate data to prove any proposition), but *all* the data on the *basis* of economic life in *all* the belligerent countries and the *whole* world.

It is precisely irrefutable summarised data of this kind that I quoted in describing the *partition of the world* in 1876 and 1914 (in Chapter VI) and the division of the world's *railways* in 1890 and 1913 (in Chapter VII). Railways are a summation of the basic capitalist industries, coal, iron and steel; a summation and the most striking index of the development of world trade and bourgeois-democratic civilisation. How the railways are linked up with large-scale industry, with monopolies, syndicates, cartels, trusts, banks and the financial oligarchy is shown in the preceding chapters of the book. The uneven distribution of the railways, their uneven development — sums up, as it were, modern monopolist capitalism on a world-wide scale. And this summary proves that imperialist wars are absolutely inevitable under *such* an economic system, *as long as* private property in the means of production exists.

The building of railways seems to be a simple, natural, democratic, cultural and civilising enterprise; that is what it is in the opinion of bourgeois professors, who are paid to depict capitalist slavery in bright colours, and in the opinion of petty-bourgeois philistines. But as a matter of fact the capitalist threads, which in thousands of different intercrossings bind these enterprises with private property in the means of production in general, have converted this railway construction into an instrument for oppressing *a thousand million* people (in the colonies and semi-colonies), that is, more than half the population of the globe that inhabit the dependent countries, as well as the wage-slaves of capital in the "civilised" countries.

Private property based on the labour of the small proprietor, free competition, democracy, all the catchwords with which the capitalists and their press deceive the workers and the peasants — are things of the distant past. Capitalism has grown into a world system of colonial oppression and of the financial strangulation of the overwhelming majority of the population of the world by a handful of "advanced" countries. And this "booty" is shared between two or three powerful world plunderers armed to the teeth (America, Great Britain, Japan), are drawing the whole world into *their* war over the sharing of *their* booty.

III

The Treaty of Brest-Litovsk[1] dictated by monarchist Germany, and the subsequent much more brutal and despicable Treaty of Versailles[2] dictated by the "democratic" republics of America and France and also by "free" Britain, have rendered a most useful service to humanity by exposing both imperialism's hired coolies of the pen and petty-bourgeois reactionaries who, although they call themselves pacifists and socialists, who sang praises to "Wilsonism,"[3] and insisted that peace and reforms were possible under imperialism.

The tens of millions of dead and maimed left by the war — a war to decide whether the British or German group of financial plunderers is to receive the most booty — and those two "peace treaties," are with unprecedented rapidity opening the eyes of the millions and tens of millions of people who are downtrodden, oppressed, deceived and duped by the bourgeoisie. Thus, out of the universal ruin caused by the war a world-wide revolutionary crisis is arising which, however prolonged and arduous its stages may be, cannot end otherwise than in a proletarian revolution and in its victory.

The Basle Manifesto of the Second International, which in 1912 gave an appraisal of the very war that broke out in 1914 and not of war in general (there are different kinds of wars, including revolutionary wars) — this Manifesto is now a monument exposing to the full the shameful bankruptcy and treachery of the heroes of the Second International.

That is why I reproduce this Manifesto as a supplement to the present edition, and again and again I urge the reader to note that the heroes of the Second International are as assiduously avoiding the passages of this Manifesto which speak precisely, clearly and definitely of the connection between that impending war and the proletarian revolution, as a thief avoids the scene of his crimes.

IV

Special attention has been devoted in this pamphlet to a criticism of Kautskyism, the international ideological trend represented in all countries of the world by the "most prominent theoreticians", the leaders of the Second International (Otto Bauer and Co. in Austria, Ramsay MacDonald and others in Britain, Albert Thomas in France, etc., etc.) and a multitude of socialists, reformists, pacifists, bourgeois-democrats and parsons.

This ideological trend is, on the one hand, a product of the disintegration and decay of the Second International, and, on the other hand, the inevitable fruit of the ideology of the petty bourgeoisie, whose entire way of life holds them captive to bourgeois and democratic prejudices.

The views held by Kautsky and his like are a complete renunciation of those same revolutionary principles of Marxism that writer has championed for decades, especially, by the way, in his struggle against socialist opportunism (of Bernstein,

Millerand, Hyndman, Gompers, etc.).[4] It is not a mere accident, therefore, that Kautsky's followers all over the world have now united in practical politics with the extreme opportunists (through the Second, or Yellow International) and with the bourgeois governments (through bourgeois coalition governments in which socialists take part).

The growing world proletarian revolutionary movement in general, and the communist movement in particular, cannot dispense with an analysis and exposure of the theoretical errors of Kautskyism. The more so since pacifism and "democracy" in general, which lay no claim to Marxism whatever, but which, like Kautsky and Co., are obscuring the profundity of the contradictions of imperialism and the inevitable revolutionary crisis to which it gives rise, are still very widespread all over the world. To combat these tendencies is the bounden duty of the party of the proletariat, which must win away from the bourgeoisie the small proprietors who are duped by them, and the millions of working people who enjoy more or less petty-bourgeois conditions of life.

V

A few words must be said about Chapter VIII "Parasitism and Decay of Capitalism". As already pointed out in the text, Hilferding, ex-"Marxist", and now a comrade-in-arms of Kautsky and one of the chief exponents of bourgeois, reformist policy in the Independent Social-Democratic Party of Germany,[5] has taken a step backward on this question compared with the *frankly* pacifist and reformist Englishman, Hobson. The international split of the entire working-class movement is now quite evident (the Second and the Third Internationals). The fact that armed struggle and civil war is now raging between the two trends is also evident — the support given to Kolchak and Denikin[6] in Russia by the Mensheviks[7] and Socialist-Revolutionaries[8] against the Bolsheviks; the fight the Scheidemanns and Noskes[9] have conducted in conjunction with the bourgeoisie against the Spartacists[10] in Germany; the same thing in Finland, Poland, Hungary, etc. What is the economic basis of this world-historic phenomenon?

It is precisely the parasitism and decay of capitalism, characteristic of its highest historical stage of development, i.e., imperialism. As this pamphlet shows, capitalism has now singled out a *handful* (less than one-tenth of the inhabitants of the globe; less than one-fifth at a most "generous" and liberal calculation) of exceptionally rich and powerful states which plunder the whole world simply by "clipping coupons". Capital exports yield an income of eight to 10 billion francs per annum, at pre-war prices and according to pre-war bourgeois statistics. Now, of course, they yield much more.

Obviously, out of such enormous *superprofits* (since they are obtained over and above the profits which capitalists squeeze out of the workers of their "own" country) it is *possible to bribe* the labour leaders and the upper stratum of the labour aristocracy. And that is just what the capitalists of the "advanced" countries are doing; they are bribing them in a thousand different ways, direct and indirect, overt and covert.

This stratum of workers-turned-bourgeois, or the labour aristocracy, who are quite philistine in their mode of life, in the size of their earnings and in their entire outlook, is the principal prop of the Second International, and, in our days, the principal *social* (not military) *prop of the bourgeoisie*. For they are the real *agents of the bourgeoisie in the working-class* movement, the labour lieutenants of the capitalist class, real vehicles of reformism and chauvinism. In the civil war between the proletariat and the bourgeoisie they inevitably, and in no small numbers, take the side of the bourgeoisie, the "Versaillais" against the "Communards".[11]

Unless the economic roots of this phenomenon are understood and its political and social significance is appreciated, not a step can be taken toward the solution of the practical problems of the communist movement and of the impending social revolution.

Imperialism is the eve of the social revolution of the proletariat. This has been confirmed since 1917 on a world-wide scale.

N. Lenin
July 6, 1920

Н. ЛЕНИНЪ (ВЛ. ИЛЬИНЪ).

ИМПЕРІАЛИЗМЪ,

КАКЪ НОВѢЙШІЙ ЭТАПЪ

КАПИТАЛИЗМА.

(Популярный очеркъ)

СКЛАДЪ ИЗДАНІЯ:
Книжный складъ и магазинъ „Жизнь и Знаніе"
Петроградъ, Поварской пер., 2, кв. 9 и 10. Тел. 227—42.
1917 г.

The cover of Imperialism, the Highest Stage of Capitalism *(1917)*

IMPERIALISM, THE HIGHEST STAGE OF CAPITALISM
A POPULAR OUTLINE

By V.I. Lenin

DURING THE LAST FIFTEEN to twenty years, especially since the Spanish-American War (1898), and the Anglo-Boer War (1899-1902), the economic and also the political literature of the two hemispheres has more and more often adopted the term "imperialism" in order to describe the present era. In 1902, a book by the English economist J. A. Hobson, *Imperialism*, was published in London and New York. This author, whose point of view is that of bourgeois social-reformism and pacifism which, in essence, is identical with the present point of view of the ex-Marxist, Karl Kautsky, gives a very good and comprehensive description of the principal specific economic and political features of imperialism. In 1910, there appeared in Vienna the work of the Austrian Marxist, Rudolf Hilferding, *Finance Capital* (Russian edition: Moscow, 1912). In spite of the mistake the author makes on the theory of money, and in spite of a certain inclination on his part to reconcile Marxism with opportunism, this work gives a very valuable theoretical analysis of "the latest phase of capitalist development," as the subtitle runs. Indeed, what has been said of imperialism during the last few years, especially in an enormous number of magazine and newspaper articles, and also in the resolutions, for example, of the Chemnitz and Basle congresses which took place in the autumn of 1912, has scarcely gone beyond the ideas expounded, or, more exactly, summed up by the two writers mentioned above …

Later on, I shall try to show briefly, and as simply as possible, the connection and relationships between the *principal* economic features of imperialism. I shall not be able to deal with the non-economic aspects of the question, however much they deserve to be dealt with. References to literature and other notes which, perhaps, would not interest all readers, are to be found at the end of this pamphlet.

I

CONCENTRATION
OF PRODUCTION AND MONOPOLIES

THE ENORMOUS GROWTH of industry and the remarkably rapid concentration of production in ever-larger enterprises are one of the most characteristic features of capitalism. Modern production censuses give most complete and most exact data on this process.

In Germany, for example, out of every 1000 industrial enterprises, large enterprises, i.e., those employing more than 50 workers, numbered three in 1882, six in 1895 and nine in 1907; and out of every 100 workers employed, this group of enterprises employed 22, 30 and 37, respectively. Concentration of production, however, is much more intense than the concentration of workers, since labour in the large enterprises is much more productive. This is shown by the figures on steam engines and electric motors. If we take what in Germany is called industry in the broad sense of the term, that is, including commerce, transport, etc., we get the following picture. Large-scale enterprises, 30,588 out of a total of 3,265,623, that is to say, 0.9%. These enterprises employ 5,700,000 workers out of a total of 14,400,000, i.e., 39.4%; they use 6,600,000 steam horsepower out of a total of 8,800,000, i.e., 75.3%, and 1,200,000 kilowatts of electricity out of a total of 1,500,000, i.e., 77.2%.

Less than one-hundredth of the total number of enterprises utilise *more than three-fourths* of the total amount of steam and electric power! Two million nine hundred and seventy thousand small enterprises (employing up to five workers), constituting 91% of the total, utilise only 7% of the total steam and electric power! Tens of thousands of huge enterprises are everything; millions of small ones are nothing.

In 1907, there were in Germany 586 establishments employing one thousand and more workers, nearly *one-tenth* (1,380,000) of the total number of workers employed in industry, and they consumed *almost one-third* (32%) of the total steam and electric power.[1] As we shall see, money capital and the banks make this superiority of a handful of the largest enterprises still more overwhelming, in the most literal sense of the word, i.e., millions of small, medium and even some big "proprietors" are in fact in complete subjection to some hundreds of millionaire financiers.

In another advanced country of modern capitalism, the United States of America, the growth of the concentration of production is still greater. Here statistics single out industry in the narrow sense of the word and classify enterprises according to the value of their annual output. In 1904 large-scale enterprises with an output valued at one million dollars and over numbered 1900 (out of 216,180, i.e., 0.9%). These employed 1,400,000 workers (out of 5,500,000, i.e., 25.6%) and the value of their output amounted to $5,600 million (out of $14,800 million, i.e., 38%). Five years later, in 1909, the corresponding figures were: 3060 enterprises (out of 268,491, i.e., 1.1%) employing two million workers (out of 6,600,000, i.e., 30.5%) with an output valued at $9 million (out of $20,700 million, i.e., 43.8%).[2]

Almost half the total production of all the enterprises of the country was carried on by *one-hundredth part* of these enterprises! These 3000 giant enterprises embrace 25 branches of industry. From this it can be seen that, at a certain stage of its development, concentration itself, as it were, leads straight to monopoly; for a score or so of giant enterprises can easily arrive at an agreement, and on the other hand, the hindrance to competition, the tendency towards monopoly, arises from the huge size of the enterprises. This transformation of competition into monopoly is one of the most important — if not the most important — phenomena of modern capitalist economy, and we must deal with it in greater detail. But first we must clear up one possible misunderstanding.

American statistics speak of 3000 giant enterprises in 250 branches of industry, as if there were only a dozen enterprises of the largest scale for each branch of industry.

But this is not the case. Not in every branch of industry are there large-scale enterprises; and moreover, a very important feature of capitalism in its highest stage of development is so-called *combination* of production, that is to say, the grouping in a single enterprise of different branches of industry, which either represent the consecutive stages in the processing of raw materials (for example, the smelting of iron ore into pig-iron, the conversion of pig-iron into steel, and then, perhaps, the manufacture of steel goods) — or are auxiliary to one another (for example, the utilisation of scrap, or of by-products, the manufacture of packing materials, etc.).

"Combination", writes Hilferding, "levels out the fluctuations of trade and therefore assures to the combined enterprises a more stable rate of profit. Secondly, combination has the effect of eliminating trade. Thirdly, it has the effect of rendering possible technical improvements, and, consequently, the acquisition of superprofits over and above those obtained by the 'pure' (i.e., non-combined) enterprises. Fourthly, it strengthens the position of the combined enterprises relative to the 'pure' enterprises, strengthens them in the competitive struggle in periods of serious depression, when the fall in prices of raw materials does not keep pace with the fall in prices of manufactured goods."[3]

The German bourgeois economist, Heymann, who has written a book especially on "mixed", that is, combined, enterprises in the German iron industry, says: "Pure enterprises perish, they are crushed between the high price of raw material and the low price of the finished product." Thus we get the following picture:

"There remain, on the one hand, the big coal companies, producing millions of tons yearly, strongly organised in their coal syndicate, and on the other, the big steel plants, closely allied to the coal mines, having their own steel syndicate. These giant enterprises, producing 400,000 tons of steel per annum, with a tremendous output of ore and coal and producing finished steel goods, employing 10,000 workers quartered in company houses, and sometimes owning their own railways and ports, are the typical representatives of the German iron and steel industry. And concentration goes on further and further. Individual enterprises are becoming larger and larger. An ever-increasing number of enterprises in one, or in several different industries, join together in giant enterprises, backed up and directed by half a dozen big Berlin banks. In relation to the German mining industry, the truth of the teachings of Karl Marx on concentration is definitely proved; true, this applies to a country where industry is protected by tariffs and freight rates. The German mining industry is ripe for expropriation.[4]

Such is the conclusion which a bourgeois economist, who, by way of exception is conscientious, had to arrive at. It must be noted that he seems to place Germany in a special category because her industries are protected by high tariffs. But this circumstance which only accelerates concentration and the formation of monopolist manufacturers' associations, cartels, syndicates, etc. It is extremely important to note that in free-trade Britain, concentration *also* leads to monopoly, although somewhat later and perhaps in another form. Professor Hermann Levy, in his special work of research entitled *Monopolies, Cartels and Trusts*, based on data on British economic development, writes as follows:

In Great Britain it is the size of the enterprise and its high technical level which harbour a monopolist tendency. This, for one thing, is due to the great investment of capital per enterprise, which gives rise to increasing demands for new capital for the new enterprises and thereby renders their launching more difficult. Moreover (and this seems to us to be the more important point) every new enterprise that wants to keep pace with the gigantic enterprises that have been formed by concentration would here produce such an enormous quantity of surplus goods that it could dispose of them only by being able to sell them profitably as a result of an enormous increase in demand; otherwise, this surplus would force prices down to a level that would be unprofitable both for the new enterprise and for the monopoly combines.

Britain differs from other countries where protective tariffs facilitate the formation of cartels in that monopolist manufacturers' associations, cartels and trusts arise in the majority of cases only when the number of the chief competing enterprises has been reduced to "a couple of dozen or so."

Here the influence of concentration on the formation of large industrial monopolies in a whole sphere of industry stands out with crystal clarity.[5]

Half a century ago, when Marx was writing *Capital*, free competition appeared to the overwhelming majority of economists to be a "natural law". Official science tried, by a conspiracy of silence, to kill the works of Marx, who by a theoretical and historical analysis of capitalism had proved that free competition gives rise to the concentration of production, which, in turn, at a certain stage of development, leads to monopoly. Today, monopoly has become a fact. Economists are writing mountains of books in which they describe the diverse manifestations of monopoly, and continue to declare in chorus that "Marxism is refuted". But facts are stubborn things, as the English proverb says, and they have to be reckoned with, whether we like it or not. The facts show that differences between capitalist countries, e.g., in the matter of protection or free trade, only give rise to insignificant variations in the form of monopolies or in the moment of their appearance; and that the rise of monopolies, as the result of the concentration of production, is a general and fundamental law of the present stage of development of capitalism.

For Europe, the time when the new capitalism *definitely* superseded the old can be established with fair precision: it was the beginning of the 20th century. In one of the latest compilations on the history of the "formation of monopolies", we read:

Isolated examples of capitalist monopoly could be cited from the period preceding 1860; in these could be discerned the embryo of the forms that are so common today; but all this undoubtedly represents the prehistory of the cartels. The real beginning of modern monopoly goes back, at the earliest, to the sixties. The first important period of development of monopoly commenced with the international industrial depression of the seventies and lasted until the beginning of the nineties ... If we examine the question on a European scale, we will find that the development of free competition reached its apex in the sixties and seventies. Then it was that Britain completed the construction of her old-style capitalist organisation. In Germany, this organisation had entered into a fierce struggle with handicraft and domestic industry, and had begun to create for itself its own forms of existence ...

The great revolution, commenced with the crash of 1873, or rather, the depression which followed it and which, with hardly discernible interruptions in the early eighties, and the unusually violent, but short-lived boom round about 1889, marks twenty-two years of European economic history ... During the short boom of 1889-90, the system of cartels was widely resorted to in order to take advantage of favorable business conditions. An ill-considered policy drove prices up still more rapidly and still higher than would have been the case if there had been no cartels, and nearly all these cartels perished ingloriously in the smash. Another five-year period of bad trade and low prices followed, but a new spirit reigned in industry; the depression was no longer regarded as something to be taken for granted: it was regarded as nothing more than a pause before another boom.

The cartel movement entered its second epoch: instead of being a transitory phenomenon, the cartels have become one of the foundations of economic life. They are winning one field of industry after another, primarily, the raw materials industry. At the beginning of the nineties the cartel system had already acquired — in the organisation of the coke syndicate on the model of which the coal syndicate was later formed — a cartel technique which has hardly been improved. For the first time the great boom at the close of the nineteenth century and the crisis of 1900-03 occurred entirely — in the mining and iron industries at least — under the aegis of the cartels. And while at that time it appeared to be something novel, now the general public takes it for granted that large spheres of economic life have been, as a general rule, removed from the realm of free competition.[6]

Thus, the principal stages in the history of monopolies are the following: (1) 1860-70, the highest stage, the apex of development of free competition; monopoly is in the barely discernible, embryonic stage. (2) After the crisis of 1873, a lengthy period of development of cartels; but they are still the exception. They are not yet durable. They are still a transitory phenomenon. (3) The boom at the end of the 19th century and the crisis of 1900-03. Cartels become one of the foundations of the whole of economic life. Capitalism has been transformed into imperialism.

Cartels come to an agreement on the terms of sale, dates of payment, etc. They divide the markets among themselves. They fix the quantity of goods to be produced. They fix prices. They divide the profits among the various enterprises, etc.

The number of cartels in Germany was estimated at about 250 in 1896 and at 385 in 1905, with about 12,000 firms participating.[7] But it is generally recognised that these figures are underestimations. From the statistics of German industry for 1907 we quoted above, it is evident that even these 12,000 very big enterprises probably consume more than half the steam and electric power used in the country. In the United States of America, the number of trusts in 1900 was estimated at 185 and in 1907, 250. American statistics divide all industrial enterprises into those belonging to individuals, to private firms or to corporations. The latter in 1904 comprised 23.6%, and in 1909, 25.9%, i.e., more than one-fourth of the total industrial enterprises in the country. These employed in 1904, 70.6%, and in 1909 75.6%, i.e., more than three-fourths of the total wage earners. Their output at these two dates was valued at $10,900 million and $16,300 million, i.e., to 73.7% and 79.0% of the total, respectively.

At times cartels and trusts concentrate in their hands seven- or eight-tenths of the total output of a given branch of industry. The Rhine-Westphalian Coal Syndicate, at its foundation in 1893, concentrated 86.7% of the total coal output of the area, and in 1910 it already concentrated 95.4%.[8] The monopoly so created assures enormous profits, and leads to the formation of technical productive units of formidable magnitude. The famous Standard Oil Company in the United States was founded in 1900:

> It has an authorised capital of $150 million. It issued $100 million common and $106 million preferred stock. From 1900 to 1907 the following dividends were paid on the latter: 48, 48, 45, 44, 36, 40, 40, 40% in the respective years, i.e., in all, $367 million. From 1882 to 1907, out of total net profits amounting to $889 million, $606 million were distributed in dividends, and the rest went to reserve capital[9] ... In 1907 the various works of the United States Steel Corporation employed no less than 210,180 people. The largest enterprise in the German mining industry, the Gelsenkirchener Bergwerksgesellschaft in 1908 had a staff of 46,048 workers and office employees.[10]

In 1902, the United States Steel Corporation already produced 9 million tons of steel.[11] Its output constituted in 1901, 66.3%, and in 1908, 56.1% of the total output of steel in the United States.[12] The output of ore was 43.9% and 46.3%, respectively.

The report of the American Government Commission on Trusts states:

> Their superiority over competitors is due to the magnitude of its enterprises and their excellent technical equipment. Since its inception, the Tobacco Trust has devoted all its efforts to the universal substitution of mechanical for manual labour. With this end in view it bought up all patents that have anything to do with the manufacture of tobacco and has spent enormous sums for this purpose. Many of these patents at first proved to be of no use, and had to be modified by the engineers employed by the

trust. At the end of 1906, two subsidiary companies were formed solely to acquire patents. With the same object in view, the trust has built its own foundries, machine shops and repair shops. One of these establishments, that in Brooklyn, employs on the average 300 workers; here experiments are carried out on inventions concerning the manufacture of cigarettes, cheroots, snuff, tinfoil for packing, boxes, etc. Here, also, inventions are perfected.[13]

Other trusts also employ so-called developing engineers whose business it is to devise new methods of production and to test technical improvements. The United States Steel Corporation grants big bonuses to its workers and engineers for all inventions that raise technical efficiency, or reduce cost of production.[14]

In German large-scale industry, e.g., in the chemical industry, which has developed so enormously during these last few decades, the promotion of technical improvement is organised in the same way. By 1908 the process of concentration of production had already given rise to two main "groups" which, in their way, were also in the nature of monopolies. At first these groups constituted "dual alliances" of two pairs of big factories, each having a capital of from 20-21 million marks — on the one hand, the former Meister Factory in Höchst and the Casella Factory in Frankfurt am Main; and on the other hand, the aniline and soda factory at Ludwigshafen and the former Bayer factory at Elberfeld. Then, in 1905, one of these groups, and in 1908 the other group, each concluded an agreement with yet another big factory. The result was the formation of two "triple alliances," each with a capital of from 40-50 million marks. And these "alliances" have already begun to "approach" each other, to reach "an understanding" about prices, etc.[15]

Competition becomes transformed into monopoly. The result is immense progress in the socialisation of production. In particular, the process of technical invention and improvement becomes socialised.

This is something quite different from the old free competition between manufacturers, scattered and out of touch with one another, and producing for an unknown market. Concentration has reached the point at which it is possible to make an approximate estimate of all sources of raw materials (for example, the iron ore deposits) of a country and even, as we shall see, of several countries, or of the whole world. Not only are such estimates made, but these sources are captured by gigantic monopolist associations. An approximate estimate of the capacity of markets is also made, and the associations "divide" them up amongst themselves by agreement. Skilled labour is monopolised, the best engineers are engaged; the means of transport are captured — railways in America, shipping companies in Europe and

America. Capitalism in its imperialist stage leads directly to the most comprehensive socialisation of production; it, so to speak, drags the capitalists, against their will and consciousness, into some sort of a new social order, a transitional one from complete free competition to complete socialisation.

Production becomes social, but appropriation remains private. The social means of production remain the private property of a few. The general framework of formally recognised free competition remains, and the yoke of a few monopolists on the rest of the population becomes a hundred times heavier, more burdensome and intolerable.

The German economist, Kestner, has written a book especially devoted to "the struggle between the cartels and outsiders", i.e., the capitalists outside the cartels. He entitled his work *Compulsory Organisation*, although, in order to present capitalism in its true light, he should, of course, have written about compulsory submission to monopolist associations. It is instructive to glance at least at the list of the methods the monopolist associations resort to in the present-day, the latest, the civilised struggle for "organisation": 1) stopping supplies of raw materials (…"one of the most important methods of compelling adherence to the cartel"); 2) stopping the supply of labour by means of "alliances" (i.e., of agreements between the capitalists and the trade unions by which the latter permit their members to work only in cartelised enterprises); 3) stopping deliveries; 4) closing trade outlets; 5) agreements with the buyers, by which the latter undertake to trade only with the cartels; 6) systematic price cutting (to ruin "outside" firms, i.e., those which refuse to submit to the monopolists. Millions are spent in order to sell goods for a certain time below their cost price; there were instances when the price of petrol was thus reduced from 40 to 22 marks, i.e., almost by half!); 7) stopping credits; 8) boycott.

Here we no longer have competition between small and large, technically developed and backward enterprises. We see here the monopolists throttling those who do not submit to them, to their yoke, to their dictation. This is how this process is reflected in the mind of a bourgeois economist:

"Even in the purely economic sphere", writes Kestner, "a certain change is taking place from commercial activity in the old sense of the word towards organisational-speculative activity. The greatest success no longer goes to the merchant whose technical and commercial experience enables him best of all to estimate the needs of the buyer and who is able to discover and, so to speak, 'awaken' a latent demand; it goes to the speculative genius" (?!) "who knows how to estimate, or even only to sense in advance the organisational development and the possibilities of certain connections between individual enterprises and the banks ..."

Translated into ordinary human language this means that the development of capitalism has arrived at a stage when, although commodity production still "reigns" and continues to be regarded as the basis of economic life, it has in reality been undermined and the bulk of the profits go to the "geniuses" of financial manipulation. At the basis of these manipulations and swindles lies socialised production; but the immense progress of mankind which achieved this socialisation, goes to benefit ... the speculators. We shall see later how "on these grounds" reactionary, petty-bourgeois critics of capitalist imperialism dream of going *back* to "free", "peaceful", and "honest" competition.

"The prolonged raising of prices which results from the formation of cartels", says Kestner, "has hitherto been observed only in respect of the most important means of production, particularly coal, iron and potassium, but never in respect of manufactured goods. Similarly, the increase in profits resulting from this raising of prices has been limited only to the industries which produce means of production. To this observation we must add that the industries which process raw materials (and not semi-manufactures) not only secure advantages from the cartel formation in the shape of high profits, to the detriment of the finished goods industry, but have also secured a *dominating position* over the latter, which did not exist under free competition."[16]

The words which I have italicised reveal the essence of the case which the bourgeois economists admit so reluctantly and so rarely, and which the present-day defenders of opportunism, led by Kautsky, so zealously try to evade and brush aside. Domination, and violence that is associated with it, such are the relationships that are typical of the "latest phase of capitalist development"; this is what inevitably had to result, and has resulted, from the formation of all-powerful economic monopolies.

I shall give one more example of the methods employed by the cartels. Where it is possible to capture all or the chief sources of raw materials, the rise of cartels and formation of monopolies is particularly easy. It would be wrong, however, to assume that monopolies do not arise in other industries in which it is impossible to corner the sources of raw materials. The cement industry, for instance, can find its raw materials everywhere. Yet in Germany this industry too is strongly cartelised. The cement manufacturers have formed regional syndicates: South German, Rhine-Westphalian, etc. The prices fixed are monopoly prices: 230 to 280 marks a car-load, when the cost price is 180 marks! The enterprises pay a dividend of from 12% to 16% — and it must not be forgotten that the "geniuses" of modern speculation know how to pocket big profits besides what they draw in dividends. In order to prevent competition in such a profitable industry, the monopolists even resort to various stratagems: they spread false rumours about the bad situation in their industry; anonymous warnings are published in the newspapers, like the following: "Capitalists, don't invest your capital in the cement industry!"; lastly, they buy up "outsiders" (those outside the syndicates) and pay them "compensation" of 60,000, 80,000 and even 150,000 marks.[17] Monopoly hews a path for itself everywhere without scruple as to the means, from paying a "modest" sum to buy off competitors to the American device of employing dynamite against them.

The statement that cartels can abolish crises is a fable spread by bourgeois economists who at all costs desire to place capitalism in a favourable light. On the contrary, the monopoly created in *certain* branches of industry, increases and intensifies the anarchy inherent in capitalist production *as a whole*. The disparity between the development of agriculture and that of industry, which is characteristic of capitalism in general, is increased. The privileged position of the most highly cartelised, so-called *heavy* industry, especially coal and iron, causes "a still greater lack of coordination" in other branches of industry — as Jeidels, the author of one of the best works on "the relationship of the German big banks to industry", admits.[18]

"The more developed an economic system is", writes Liefmann, an unblushing apologist of capitalism, "the more it resorts to risky enterprises, or enterprises in other countries, to those which need a great deal of time to develop, or finally, to those which are only of local importance".[19] The increased risk is connected in the long run with the prodigious increase of capital, which, as it were, overflows the brim, flows abroad, etc. At the same time the extremely rapid rate of technical progress gives rise to increasing elements of disparity between the various spheres of national economy, to anarchy and crises. Liefmann is obliged to admit that: "In all probability mankind will see further important technical revolutions in the near future which will also affect the organisation of the economic system" … electricity and aviation … "As a general rule, in such periods of radical economic change, speculation develops on a large scale."[20]

Crises of every kind — economic crises most frequently, but not only these — in their turn increase very considerably the tendency towards concentration and towards monopoly. In this connection, the following reflections of Jeidels on the significance of the crisis of 1900, which, as we have already seen, marked the turning point in the history of modern monopoly, are exceedingly instructive:

> Side by side with the gigantic plants in the basic industries, the crisis of 1900 still found many plants organised on lines that today would be considered obsolete, the "pure"

(non-combined) plants, which were brought into being at the height of the industrial boom. The fall in prices and the falling off in demand put these "pure" enterprises in a precarious position, which did not affect the gigantic combined enterprises at all or only affected them for a very short time. As a consequence of this the crisis of 1900 resulted in a far greater concentration of industry than the crisis of 1873: the latter crisis also produced a sort of selection of the best-equipped enterprises, but owing to the level of technical development at that time, this selection could not place the firms which successfully emerged from the crisis in a position of monopoly. Such a durable monopoly exists to a high degree in the gigantic enterprises in the modern iron and steel and electrical industries owing to their very complicated technique, far-reaching organisation and magnitude of capital, and, to a lesser degree, in the engineering industry, certain branches of the metallurgical industry, transport, etc.[21]

Monopoly! This is the last word in the "latest phase of capitalist development." But we shall only have a very insufficient, incomplete, and poor notion of the real power and the significance of modern monopolies if we do not take into consideration the part played by the banks. +

II

BANKS AND THEIR NEW ROLE

THE PRINCIPAL AND PRIMARY function of banks is to serve as middlemen in the making of payments. In so doing they transform inactive money capital into active, that is, into capital yielding a profit; they collect all kinds of money revenues and place them at the disposal of the capitalist class.

As banking develops and becomes concentrated in a small number of establishments, the banks grow from modest middlemen into powerful monopolies having at their command almost the whole of the money capital of all the capitalists and small businessmen and also the larger part of the means of production and sources of raw materials in any one country and in a number of countries. This transformation of numerous modest middlemen into a handful of monopolists is one of the fundamental processes in the growth of capitalism into capitalist imperialism; for this reason we must first of all examine the concentration of banking.

In 1907-08, the combined deposits of the German joint stock banks, each having a capital of more than a million marks, amounted to 7 billion marks; in 1912-13, these deposits already amounted to 9800 million marks, i.e., an increase of 40% in five years; and of the 2800 million increase, 2750 million was divided amongst 57 banks, each having a capital of more than 10 million marks. The distribution of the deposits between big and small banks was as follows:[22]

	In 9 big Berlin banks	Percentage of Total Deposits		
		In the other 48 banks with a capital of more than 10 million marks	In 115 banks with a capital of 1-10 million marks	In small banks (with a capital of less than 1 million marks)
1907-08	47	32.5	16.5	4
1912-13	49	36	12	3

The small banks are being squeezed out by the big banks, of which only nine concentrate in their hands almost half the total deposits. But we have left out of account many important details, for instance, the transformation of numerous small banks into actual branches of the big banks, etc. Of this I shall speak later on.

At the end of 1913, Schulze-Gaevernitz estimated the deposits in the nine big Berlin banks at 5100 million marks, out of a total of about 10 billion marks. Taking into account not only the deposits, but the total bank capital, this author wrote:

> At the end of 1909, the nine big Berlin banks, *together with their affiliated banks*, controlled 11,300 million marks, that is, about 83% of the total German bank capital. The Deutsche Bank, which *together with its affiliated banks* controls nearly 3000 million marks, represents, parallel to the Prussian State Railway Administration, the biggest and also the most decentralised accumulation of capital in the Old World.[23]

I have emphasised the reference to the "affiliated" banks because it is one of the most important distinguishing features of modern capitalist concentration. The big enterprises and the banks in particular, not only completely absorb the small ones, but also "annex" them, subordinate them, bring them into their "own" group or "concern" (to use the technical term) by acquiring "holdings" in their capital, by purchasing or exchanging shares, by a system of credits, etc., etc. Professor Liefmann has written a voluminous "work" of about 500 pages describing modern "holding and finance companies",[24] unfortunately adding very dubious "theoretical" reflections to what is frequently undigested raw material. To what results this "holding" system leads in respect of concentration is best illustrated in the book written on the big German banks by Riesser, himself a banker. But before examining his data, let us quote a concrete example of the "holding" system.

The Deutsche Bank "group" is one of the biggest, if not the biggest, of the big banking groups. In order to trace the main threads which connect all the banks in this group, a distinction must be made between "holdings" of the first, second and third degree, or what amounts to the same thing, between dependence (of the lesser banks on the Deutsche Bank) in the first, second and third degree. We then obtain the following picture:[25]

The Deutsche Bank has holdings		Direct or 1st degree dependence	2nd degree dependence	3rd degree dependence
	Permanently	in 17 other banks	9 of the 17 have holdings in 34 other banks	4 of the 9 have holdings in 7 other banks
	For an indefinite period	in 5 other banks	-	-
	Occasionally	in 8 other banks	5 of the 8 have holdings in 14 other banks	2 of the 5 have holdings in 2 other banks
	Totals	in 30 other banks	14 of the 30 have holdings in 48 other banks	6 of the 14 have holdings in 9 other banks

Included in the eight banks "occasionally" dependent on the Deutsche Bank in the "first degree", "occasionally", are three foreign banks: one Austrian (the Wiener Bankverein) and two Russian (the Siberian Commercial Bank and the Russian Bank for Foreign Trade). Altogether, the Deutsche Bank group comprises, directly and indirectly, partially and totally, 87 banks; and the total capital — its own and that of others which it controls — is estimated at between two and three billion marks.

It is obvious that a bank which stands at the head of such a group, and which enters into agreement with half a dozen other banks only slightly smaller than itself for the purpose of conducting exceptionally big and profitable financial operations like floating state loans, has already outgrown the part of "middleman" and has become a association of a handful of monopolists.

The rapidity with which the concentration of banking proceeded in Germany at the turn of the 20th century is shown by the following data which we quote in an abbreviated form from Riesser:

Six Big Berlin Banks

	Branches in Germany	Deposit banks and exchange offices	Constant holdings in German joint-stock banks	Total establish-ments
1895	16	14	1	42
1900	21	40	8	80
1911	104	276	63	450

We see the rapid expansion of a close network of channels which cover the whole country, centralising all capital and all revenues, transforming thousands and thousands of scattered economic enterprises into a single national capitalist, and then into a world capitalist economy. The "decentralisation" that Schulze-Gaevernitz, as an exponent of present-day bourgeois political economy, speaks of in the passage previously quoted, really means the subordination to a single centre of an increasing number of formerly relatively "independent", or rather, strictly local economic units. In reality it is *centralisation*, the enhancement of the role, importance and power of monopolist giants.

In the older capitalist countries this "banking network" is still more close. In Great Britain and Ireland, in 1910, there were in all 7151 branches of banks. Four big banks had more than 400 branches each (from 447 to 689); four had more than 200 branches each, and eleven more than 100 each.

In France, *three* very big banks, Crédit Lyonnais, the Comptoir National and the Société Générale, extended their operations and their network of branches in the following manner.[26]

	Number of branches and offices			Capital (in million francs)	
	In the provinces	In Paris	Total	Own capital	Deposits used as capital
1870	47	17	64	200	427
1890	192	66	258	265	1245
1909	1033	196	1229	887	4363

In order to show the "connections" of a big modern bank, Riesser gives the following figures of the number of letters dispatched and received by the Disconto-Gesellschaft, one of the biggest banks in Germany and in the world (its capital in 1914 amounted to 300 million marks):

	Letters received	Letters dispatched
1852	6,135	6,292
1870	85,800	87,513
1900	533,102	626,043

The number of accounts of the big Paris bank, the Crédit Lyonnais, increased from 28,535 in 1875 to 633,539 in 1912.[27]

These simple figures show perhaps better than lengthy disquisitions how the concentration of capital and the growth of bank turnover are radically changing the significance of the banks. Scattered capitalists are transformed into a single collective capitalist. When carrying the current accounts of a few capitalists, a bank, as it were, transacts a purely technical and exclusively auxiliary operation. When, however, this operation grows to enormous dimensions we find that a handful of monopolists subordinate to their will all the operations, both commercial and industrial, of the whole of capitalist society; for they are enabled — by means of their banking connections, their current accounts and other financial operations — first, to *ascertain exactly* the financial position of the various capitalists, then to *control* them, to influence them by restricting or enlarging, facilitating or hindering credits, and finally to *entirely determine* their fate, determine their income, deprive them of capital, or permit them to increase their capital rapidly and to enormous dimensions, etc.

We have just mentioned the 300 million marks capital of the Disconto-Gesellschaft of Berlin. This increase of the capital of the bank was one of the incidents in the struggle for hegemony between two of the biggest Berlin banks — the Deutsche Bank and the Disconto. In 1870, the first was still a novice and had a capital of only 15 million marks, while the second had a capital of 30 million marks. In 1908, the first had a capital of 200 million, while the second had 170 million. In 1914 the first increased its capital to 250 million and the second, by merging with another first-class big bank, the Schaaffhausenscher Bankverein, increased its capital to 300 million. And of course, this struggle for hegemony went hand in hand with the more and more frequent conclusion of "agreements" of an increasingly durable character between the two banks. The following are the conclusions that this development of banking forces upon banking specialists who regard economic questions from a standpoint which does not in the least exceed the bounds of the most moderate and cautious bourgeois reformism.

Commenting on the increase of the capital of the Disconto-Gesellschaft to 300 million marks, the German review, *Die Bank*, wrote:

> Other banks will follow this same path and in time the 300 men, who today govern Germany economically, will gradually be reduced to 50, 25 or still fewer. It cannot be expected that this latest move towards concentration will be confined to banking. The close relations that exist between individual banks naturally lead to the bringing together of the industrial syndicates which these banks favour … One fine morning we shall wake up in surprise to see nothing but trusts before our eyes, and to find ourselves faced with the necessity of substituting state monopolies for private monopolies. However, we have nothing to reproach ourselves with, except that we have allowed things to follow their own course, slightly accelerated by the manipulation of stocks.[28]

This is an example of the impotence of bourgeois journalism which differs from bourgeois science only in that the latter is less sincere and strives to obscure the essence of the matter, to hide the forest behind the trees. To be "surprised" at the results of concentration, to "reproach" the government of capitalist Germany, or capitalist "society" ("ourselves"), to fear that the introduction of stocks and shares might "accelerate" concentration in the same way as the German "cartel" specialist Tschierschky fears the American trusts and "prefers" the German cartels on the grounds that they "may not, like the trusts, excessively accelerate technical and economic progress"[29] — is not this impotence?

But facts remain facts. There are no trusts in Germany; there are "only" cartels — but Germany is *governed* by not more than 300 magnates of capital, and the number of these is constantly diminishing. At all events, banks greatly intensify and accelerate the process of concentration of capital and the formation of monopolies in all capitalist countries, notwithstanding all the differences in their banking laws.

The banking system "possesses indeed the form of universal book-keeping and the distribution of means of production on a social scale, but solely the form," wrote Marx in *Capital* half a century ago (Russ. trans. Vol. III, part II, p. 144). The figures we have quoted on the growth of bank capital, on the increase in the number of the branches and offices of the biggest banks, the increase in the number of their accounts, etc., present a concrete picture of this "universal book-keeping" of the *whole* capitalist class; and not only of the capitalists, for the banks collect, even though temporarily, all kinds of money revenues — of small businessmen, office clerks, and of a tiny upper stratum of the working class. "Universal distribution of means of production" — that, from the formal aspect, is what *grows* out of the modern banks, which numbering some three to six of the biggest in France, and six to eight in Germany, control millions and millions. In *substance*, however, the distribution of means of production is not at all "universal", but private, i.e., it conforms to the interests of big capital, and primarily, of huge, monopoly capital, which operates under conditions in which the masses live in want, in which the whole development of agriculture hopelessly lags behind the development of industry, while within industry itself the "heavy industries" exact tribute from all other branches of industry.

In the matter of socialising capitalist economy the savings banks and post offices are beginning to compete with the banks; they are more "decentralised", i.e., their influence extends to a greater number of localities, to more remote places, to wider sections of the population. Here is the data collected by an American commission on the comparative growth of deposits in banks and savings banks:[30]

| | Deposits (in billions of marks) | | | | | |
| | Britain | | France | | Germany | | |
	Banks	Savings banks	Banks	Savings banks	Banks	Credit societies	Savings banks
1880	8.4	1.6	?	0.9	0.5	0.4	2.6
1888	12.4	2.0	1.5	2.1	1.1	0.4	4.5
1908	23.2	4.2	3.7	4.2	7.1	2.2	13.9

As they pay interest at the rate of 4% and 4.25% on deposits, the savings banks must seek "profitable" investments for their capital, they must deal in bills, mortgages, etc. The boundaries between the banks and the savings banks "become more and more obliterated". The Chambers of Commerce of Bochum and Erfurt, for example, demand that savings banks be "prohibited" from engaging in "purely" banking business, such as discounting bills; they demand the limitation of the "banking" operations of the post office.[31] The banking magnates seem to be afraid that state monopoly will steal upon them from an unexpected quarter. It goes without saying, however, that this fear is no more than an expression of the rivalry, so to speak, between two department managers in the same office; for, on the one hand, the millions entrusted to the savings-banks are in the final analysis actually controlled by *these very same* bank capital magnates, while, on the other hand, state monopoly in capitalist society is merely a means of increasing and guaranteeing the income of millionaires in some branch of industry who are on the verge of bankruptcy.

The change from the old type of capitalism, in which free competition predominated, to the new capitalism, in which monopoly reigns, is expressed, among other things, by a decline in the importance of the Stock Exchange. The review, *Die Bank*, writes: "The Stock Exchange has long ceased to be the indispensable medium of circulation that it formerly was when the banks were not yet able to place the bulk of new issues with their clients."[32]

"'Every bank is a Stock Exchange,' and the bigger the bank, and the more successful the concentration of banking, the truer does this modern aphorism ring."[33] "While formerly, in the seventies, the Stock Exchange, flushed with the exuberance of youth" (a "subtle" allusion to the Stock Exchange crash of 1873, the company promotion scandals, etc.), "opened the era of the industrialisation of Germany, nowadays the banks and industry are able to 'manage it alone.' The domination of our big banks over the Stock Exchange ... is nothing else than the expression of the completely organised German industrial state. If the domain of the automatically functioning economic laws is thus restricted, and if the domain of conscious regulation by the banks is considerably enlarged, the national economic responsibility of a few guiding heads is immensely increased", so writes the German professor Schulze-Gaevernitz,[34] an apologist of German imperialism, who is regarded as an authority by the imperialists of all countries, and who tries to gloss over the mere "detail" that the "conscious regulation" of economic life by the banks consists in the fleecing of the public by a handful of "completely organised" monopolists. The task of a bourgeois professor is not to lay bare the entire mechanism, or to expose all the machinations of the bank monopolists, but rather to present them in a favourable light.

In the same way, Riesser, a still more authoritative economist and himself a banker, makes shift with meaningless phrases in order to explain away undeniable facts:

> ... the Stock Exchange is steadily losing the feature which is absolutely essential for
> national economy as a whole and for the circulation of securities in particular — that
> of being not only a most exact measuring-rod, but also an almost automatic regulator
> of the economic movements which converge on it.[35]

In other words, the old capitalism, the capitalism of free competition with its indispensable regulator, the Stock Exchange, is passing away. A new capitalism has come to take its place, bearing obvious features of something transient, a mixture of free competition and monopoly. The question naturally arises: *into what* is this new capitalism "developing"? But the bourgeois scholars are afraid to raise this question.

"Thirty years ago, businessmen, freely competing against one another, performed nine-tenths of the work connected with their business other than manual labour. At the present time, nine-tenths of this 'brain work' is performed by *employees*. Banking is in the forefront of this evolution."[36] This admission by Schulze-Gaevernitz brings us once again to the question: to what is this new capitalism, capitalism in its imperialist stage, developing?

Among the few banks which remain at the head of all capitalist economy as a result of the process of concentration, there is naturally to be observed an increasingly marked tendency towards monopolist agreements, towards a *bank trust*. In America, not nine, but *two* very big banks, those of the billionaires Rockefeller and Morgan, control a capital of 11 billion marks.[37] In Germany the absorption of the Schaaffhausenscher Bankverein by the Disconto-Gesellschaft to which I referred above, was commented on in the following terms by the *Frankfurter Zeitung*, an organ of Stock Exchange interests:

> The concentration movement of the banks is narrowing the circle of establishments
> from which it is possible to obtain credits, and is consequently increasing the dependence

of big industry upon a small number of banking groups. In view of the close connection between industry and the financial world, the freedom of movement of industrial companies which need banking capital is restricted. For this reason, big industry is watching the growing trustification of the banks with mixed feelings. Indeed, we have repeatedly seen the beginnings of certain agreements between the individual big banking concerns, which aim at restricting competition.[38]

Again and again, the final word in the development of banking is monopoly.

As regards the close connection between the banks and industry, it is precisely in this sphere that the new role of the banks is, perhaps, most strikingly felt. When a bank discounts a bill for a firm, opens a current account for it, etc., these operations, taken separately, do not in the least diminish its independence, and the bank plays no other part than that of a modest middleman. But when such operations are multiplied and become an established practice, when the bank "collects" in its own hands enormous amounts of capital, when the running of a current account for a given firm enables the bank — and this is what happens — to obtain fuller and more detailed information about the economic position of its client, the result is that the industrial capitalist becomes more completely dependent on the bank.

At the same time a personal link-up, so to speak, is established between the banks and the biggest industrial and commercial enterprises, the merging of one with another through the acquisition of shares, through the appointment of bank directors to the supervisory boards (or boards of directors) of industrial and commercial enterprises, and vice versa. The German economist, Jeidels, has compiled most detailed data on this form of concentration of capital and of enterprises. Six of the biggest Berlin banks were represented by their directors in *344* industrial companies; and by their board members in *407* others, making a total of *751* companies. In *289* of these companies they either had two of their representatives on each of the respective supervisory boards, or held the posts of chairmen. We find these industrial and commercial companies in the most diverse branches of industry: insurance, transport, restaurants, theaters, art industry, etc. On the other hand, on the supervisory boards of these six banks (in 1910) were 51 of the biggest industrialists, including the director of Krupp, of the powerful "Hapag" (Hamburg-American Line), etc., etc. From 1895 to 1910, each of these six banks participated in the share and bond issues of many hundreds of industrial companies (the number ranging from 281 to 419).[39]

The "personal link-up" between the banks and industry is supplemented by the "personal link-up" between both of them and the government. "Seats on supervisory boards," writes Jeidels, "are freely offered to persons of title, also to ex-civil servants, who are able to do a great deal to facilitate [!!] relations with the authorities ... Usually, on the supervisory board of a big bank, there is a member of parliament or a Berlin city councillor."

The building and development, so to speak, of the big capitalist monopolies is therefore going on full steam ahead in all "natural" and "supernatural" ways. A sort of division of labour is being systematically developed amongst the several hundreds of kings of finance who reign over modern capitalist society:

> Simultaneously with this widening of the sphere of activity of certain big industrialists [joining the boards of banks, etc.] and with the assignment of provincial bank managers to definite industrial regions, there is a growth of specialisation among the directors of the big banks. Generally speaking, this specialisation is only conceivable when banking is conducted on a large scale, and particularly when it has widespread connections with industry. This division of labour proceeds along two lines: on the one hand, relations with industry as a whole are entrusted to one director, as his special function; on the other, each director assumes the supervision of several separate enterprises, or of a group of enterprises in the same branch of industry or having similar interests ... [Capitalism has already reached the stage of organised *supervision* of individual enterprises.] One specialises in German industry, sometimes even in West German industry alone [the West is the most industrialised part of Germany], others specialise in relations with foreign states and foreign industry, in information on the characters of industrialists and others, in Stock Exchange questions, etc. Besides, each bank director is often assigned a special locality or a special branch of industry; one works chiefly on supervisory boards of electric companies, another on chemical, brewing, or beet-sugar plants, a third in a few isolated industrial enterprises, but at the same time works on the supervisory boards of insurance companies ... In short, there can be no doubt that the growth in the dimensions and diversity of the big banks' operations is accompanied by an increase in the division of labour among their directors with the object (and result) of, so to speak, lifting them somewhat out of pure banking and making them better experts, better judges of the general problems of industry and the special problems of each branch of industry, thus making them more capable of acting within the respective bank's industrial sphere of influence. This system is supplemented by the banks' endeavours to elect to their supervisory boards men who are experts in industrial affairs, such as industrialists, former officials, especially those formerly in the railway service or in mining ...[40]

We find the same system only in a slightly different form in French banking. For instance, one of the three biggest French banks, the Crédit Lyonnais, has organised a financial research service (*service des études financières*), which permanently employs over 50 engineers, statisticians, economists, lawyers, etc. This costs from six to seven million francs annually. The service is in turn divided into eight departments: one specialises in collecting information on industrial establishments, another studies general statistics, a third railway and steamship companies, a fourth, securities, a fifth, financial reports, etc.[41]

The result is, on the one hand, the ever growing merger, or, as N. I. Bukharin aptly calls it, coalescence, of bank and industrial capital and, on the other hand, the growth of the banks into institutions of a truly "universal character". On this question I think it necessary to quote the exact terms used by Jeidels, who has best studied the subject:

> An examination of the sum total of industrial relationships reveals the universal *character* of the financial establishments working on behalf of industry. Unlike other kinds of banks, and contrary to the demand sometimes expressed in literature that banks should specialise in one kind of business or in one branch of industry in order to prevent the ground from slipping from under their feet — the big banks are striving to make their connections with industrial enterprises as varied as possible in respect of the locality or branches of industry and are striving to eliminate the unevenness in the distribution of capital among localities and branches of industry resulting from the historical development of individual enterprises ... One tendency is to make the connections with industry general; another tendency is to make them durable and close. In the six big banks both these tendencies are realised, not in full, but to a considerable extent and to an equal degree.

Quite often industrial and commercial circles complain of the "terrorism" of the banks. And it is not surprising that such complaints are heard, for the big banks "command", as will be seen from the following example. On November 19, 1901, one of the big, so-called Berlin "D" banks (the names of the four biggest banks begin with the letter D) wrote to the Board of Directors of the German Central Northwest Cement Syndicate in the following terms:

> As we learn from the notice you published in a certain newspaper of the 18th inst., we must reckon with the possibility that the next general meeting of your syndicate, to be held on the 30th of this month, may decide on measures which are likely to effect changes in your undertaking which are unacceptable to us. We deeply regret that, for these reasons, we are obliged henceforth to withdraw the credit which had hitherto been allowed you ... But if the said next general meeting does not decide upon measures which are unacceptable to us, and if we receive suitable guarantees on this matter for

the future, we shall be quite willing to open negotiations with you on the grant of a new credit.[42]

As a matter of fact, this is small capital's old complaint about being oppressed by big capital, but in this case it was a whole syndicate that fell into the category of "small" capital! The old struggle between small and big capital is being resumed at a new and immeasurably higher stage of development. It stands to reason that the big banks' enterprises, worth many millions, can accelerate technical progress with means that cannot possibly be compared with those of the past. The banks, for example, set up special technical research societies, and, of course, only "friendly" industrial enterprises benefit from their work. To this category belong the Electric Railway Research Association, the Central Bureau of Scientific and Technical Research, etc.

The directors of the big banks themselves cannot fail to see that new conditions of national economy are being created; but they are powerless in the face of these phenomena.

"Anyone who has watched, in recent years", writes Jeidels, "the changes of incumbents of directorships and seats on the supervisory boards of the big banks, cannot fail to have noticed that power is gradually passing into the hands of men who consider the active intervention of the big banks in the general development of industry to be necessary and of increasing importance. Between these new men and the old bank directors, disagreements on this subject of a business and often of a personal nature are growing. The issue is whether or not the banks, as credit institutions, will suffer from this intervention in industry, whether they are sacrificing tried principles and an assured profit to engage in a field of activity which has nothing in common with their role as middlemen in providing credit, and which is leading the banks into a field where they are more than ever before exposed to the blind forces of trade fluctuations. This is the opinion of many of the older bank directors, while most of the young men consider active intervention in industry to be a necessity as great as that which gave rise, simultaneously with big modern industry, to the big banks and modern industrial banking. The two parties are agreed only on one point: that there are neither firm principles nor a concrete aim in the new activities of the big banks."[43]

The old capitalism has had its day. The new capitalism represents a transition towards something. It is hopeless, of course, to seek for "firm principles and a concrete aim" for the purpose of "reconciling" monopoly with free competition. The admission of the practical men has quite a different ring from the official praises of the charms of "organised" capitalism sung by its apologists, Schulze-Gaevernitz, Liefmann and similar "theoreticians".

At precisely what period were the "new activities" of the big banks finally established? Jeidels gives us a fairly exact answer to this important question:

The connections between the banks and industrial enterprises, with their new content, their new forms and their new organs, namely, the big banks which are organised on both a centralised and a decentralised basis, were scarcely a characteristic economic phenomenon before the nineties; in one sense, indeed this initial date may be advanced to the year 1897, when the important "mergers" took place and when, for the first time, the new form of decentralised organisation was introduced to suit the industrial policy of the banks. This starting-point could perhaps be placed at an even later date, for it was the crisis of 1900 that enormously accelerated and intensified the process of concentration of industry and of banking, consolidated that process, for the first time transformed the connection with industry into the actual monopoly of the big banks, and made this connection much closer and more active.[44]

Thus, the 20th century marks the turning point from the old capitalism to the new, from the domination of capital in general to the domination of finance capital. +

III

FINANCE CAPITAL AND THE FINANCIAL OLIGARCHY

"A STEADILY INCREASING proportion of capital in industry", writes Hilferding, "ceases to belong to the industrialists who employ it. They obtain the use of it only through the medium of the banks which, in relation to them, represent the owners of the capital. On the other hand, the bank is forced to sink an increasing share of its funds in industry. Thus, to an ever greater degree the banker is being transformed into an industrial capitalist. This bank capital, i.e., capital in money form, which is thus actually transformed into industrial capital, I call 'finance capital' ... Finance capital is capital controlled by banks and employed by industrialists."[45]

This definition is incomplete in so far as it is silent on one extremely important fact — on the increase of concentration of production and of capital to such an extent that concentration is leading, and has led, to monopoly. But throughout the whole of his work, and particularly in the two chapters preceding the one from which this definition is taken Hilferding stresses the part played by *capitalist monopolies*.

The concentration of production; the monopolies arising therefrom; the merging or coalescence of the banks with industry — such is the history of the rise of finance capital and such is the content of that concept.

We now have to describe how, under the general conditions of commodity production and private property, the "business operations" of capitalist monopolies inevitably lead to the domination of a financial oligarchy. It should be noted that German — and not only German — bourgeois scholars, like Riesser, Schulze-Gaevernitz, Liefmann and others, are all apologists of imperialism and of finance capital. Instead of revealing the "mechanics" of the formation of an oligarchy, its methods, the size of its revenues "impeccable and peccable", its connections with parliaments, etc., etc., they obscure or gloss over them. They evade these "vexed questions" by pompous and vague phrases, appeals to the "sense of responsibility" of bank directors, by praising "the sense of duty" of Prussian officials, giving serious study to the petty details of absolutely ridiculous parliamentary bills for the "supervision" and "regulation" of monopolies, playing spillikins with theories, like, for example, the following "scholarly" definition, arrived at by Professor Liefmann: *"Commerce is an occupation having for its object the collection, storage and supply of goods."*[46] (The professor's bold-face italics.) ... From this it would follow that commerce existed in the time of primitive man, who knew nothing about exchange, and that it will exist under socialism!

But the monstrous facts concerning the monstrous rule of the financial oligarchy are so glaring that in all capitalist countries, in America, France and Germany, a whole literature has sprung up, written from the *bourgeois* point of view, but which, nevertheless, gives a fairly truthful picture and criticism — petty-bourgeois, naturally — of this oligarchy.

Paramount importance attaches to the "holding system", already briefly referred to above. The German economist, Heymann, probably the first to call attention to this matter, describes the essence of it in this way:

The head of the concern controls the principal company [literally: the "mother company"]; the latter reigns over the subsidiary companies ["daughter companies"] which in their turn control still other subsidiaries ["grandchild companies"], etc. In this way, it is possible with a comparatively small capital to dominate immense spheres of production. Indeed, if holding 50% of the capital is always sufficient to control a company, the head of the concern needs only one million to control eight million in the second subsidiaries. And if this "interlocking" is extended, it is possible with one million to control 16 million, 32 million, etc.[47]

As a matter of fact, experience shows that it is sufficient to own 40% of the shares of a company in order to direct its affairs,[48] since in practice a certain number of small, scattered shareholders find it impossible to attend general meetings, etc. The "democratisation" of the ownership of shares, from which the bourgeois sophists and opportunist so-called "Social-Democrats" expect (or say that they expect) the "democratisation of capital", the strengthening of the role and significance of small-scale production, etc., is, in fact, one of the ways of increasing the power of the financial oligarchy. Incidentally, this is why, in the more advanced, or in the older and more "experienced" capitalist countries, the law allows the issue of shares of smaller denomination. In Germany, the law does not permit the issue of shares of less than 1000 marks denomination, and the magnates of German finance look with an envious eye at Britain, where the issue of one-pound shares (= 20 marks, about 10 rubles) is permitted. Siemens, one of the biggest industrialists and "financial kings" in Germany, told the Reichstag on June 7, 1900, that "the one-pound share is the basis of British imperialism".[49] This merchant has a much deeper and more "Marxist" understanding of imperialism than a certain disreputable writer who is held to be one of the founders of Russian Marxism and believes that imperialism is a bad habit of a certain nation...

But the "holding system" not only serves enormously to increase the power of the monopolists; it also enables them to resort with impunity to all sorts of shady and dirty tricks to cheat the public, because formally the directors of the "mother company" are not legally responsible for the "daughter company", which is supposed to be "independent", and *through the medium* of which they can "pull off" *anything*. Here is an example taken from the German review, *Die Bank*, for May 1914:

> The Spring Steel Company of Kassel was regarded some years ago as being one of the most profitable enterprises in Germany. Through bad management its dividends fell from 15% to nil. It appears that the Board, without consulting the shareholders, had loaned *six million marks* to one of its "daughter companies", the Hassia Company, which had a nominal capital of only some hundreds of thousands of marks. This commitment, amounting to nearly treble the capital of the "mother company", was never mentioned in its balance-sheets. This omission was quite legal and could be hushed up for two whole years because it did not violate any point of company law. The chairman of the supervisory board, who as the responsible head had signed the false balance-sheets, was, and still is, the president of the Kassel Chamber of Commerce. The shareholders only heard of the loan to the Hassia Company, long afterwards, when it had been proved to be a mistake [the writer should put this word in quotation marks] and when Spring Steel shares dropped nearly 100%, because those in the know were getting rid of them...

> *This typical example of balance-sheet jugglery, quite common* in joint-stock companies, explains why their boards of directors are willing to undertake risky transactions with a far lighter heart than individual businessmen. Modern methods of drawing up balance-sheets not only make it possible to conceal doubtful undertakings from the ordinary shareholder, but also allow the people most concerned to escape the consequence of unsuccessful speculation by selling their shares in time while the individual businessman risks his own skin in everything he does...

> The balance-sheets of many joint-stock companies put us in mind of the palimpsests of the Middle Ages from which the visible inscription had first to be erased in order to discover beneath it another inscription giving the real meaning of the document. [Palimpsests are parchment documents from which the original inscription has been

erased and another inscription imposed.]

The simplest and, therefore, most common procedure for making balance sheets indecipherable is to divide a single business into several parts by setting up "daughter companies" — or by annexing them. The advantages of this system for various purposes — legal and illegal — are so evident that big companies which do not employ it are quite the exception.[50]

As an example of a huge monopolist company that extensively employs this system, the author quotes the famous General Electric Company (the AEG, to which we shall refer again later on). In 1912, it was calculated that this company held shares in *175* to *200* other companies, dominating them, of course, and thus controlling a total capital of about *1500 million marks*.[51]

None of the rules of control, the publication of balance-sheets, the drawing up of balance sheets according to a definite form, the public auditing of accounts, etc., the things about which well-intentioned professors and officials — that is, those imbued with the good intention of defending and prettyfying capitalism — discourse to the public, are of any avail; for private property is sacred, and no one can be prohibited from buying, selling, exchanging or hypothecating shares, etc.

The extent to which this "holding system" has developed in the big Russian banks may be judged by the figures given by E. Agahd, who for 15 years was an official of the Russo-Chinese Bank and who, in May 1914 published a book, not altogether correctly entitled *Big Banks and the World Market*.[52] The author divides the big Russian banks into two main groups: a) banks that come under the "holding system", and b) "independent" banks — "independence", however, being arbitrarily taken to mean independence of *foreign* banks. The author divides the first group into three sub-groups: 1) German holdings, 2) British holdings, and 3) French holdings, having in view the "holdings" and domination of the big foreign banks of the particular country mentioned. The author divides the capital of the banks into "productively" invested capital (industrial and commercial undertakings), and "speculatively" invested capital (in Stock Exchange and financial operations), assuming, from his petty-bourgeois reformist point of view, that it is possible, under capitalism, to separate the first form of investment from the second and to abolish the second form.

Here are the figures he supplies:

Bank Assets
(According to Reports for October-November, 1913)

Groups of Russian Banks	Capital invested (in millions of rubles)		
	Productively	Speculatively	Total
a 1) Four banks: Siberian Commercial, Russian, International, and Discount Bank 413.7		859.1	1272.8
a 2) Two banks: Commercial and Industrial, and Russo-British 239.3		169.1	408.4
a 3) Five banks: Russian-Asiatic, St. Petersburg Private, Azov-Don, Union Moscow, Russo-French Commercial... 711.8		661.2	1373.0
(11 banks) Total: a) =	1364.8	1689.4	3054.2
b) Eight banks: Moscow Merchants, Volga-Kama, Junker and Co., St. Petersburg Commercial (formerly Wawelberg), Bank of Moscow (formerly Ryabushinsky), Moscow Discount, Moscow Commercial, Moscow Private 504.2		391.1	895.3
(19 banks) Total:	1869.0	2080.5	3949.5

According to these figures, of the approximately four billion rubles making up the "working" capital of the big banks, *more than three-fourths*, more than three billion, belonged to banks which in reality were only "daughter companies" of foreign banks, and chiefly of Paris banks (the famous trio: Union Parisienne, Paris et Pays-Bas and Société Générale), and of Berlin banks (particularly the Deutsche Bank and Disconto-Gesellschaft). Two of the biggest Russian banks, the Russian (Russian Bank for Foreign Trade) and the International (St. Petersburg International Commercial Bank), between 1906 and 1912 increased their capital from 44 to 98 million rubles, and their reserves from 15 million to 39 million "employing three-fourths German capital". The first bank belongs to the Berlin Deutsche Bank "concern" and the second to the Berlin Disconto-Gesellschaft. The worthy Agahd is deeply indignant at the majority of the shares being held by the Berlin banks, so that the Russian shareholders are, therefore, powerless. Naturally, the country which exports capital skims the cream: for example, the Berlin Deutsche Bank, before placing the shares of the Siberian Commercial Bank on the Berlin market, kept them in its portfolio for a whole year, and then sold them at the rate of 193 for 100, that is, at nearly twice their nominal value, "earning" a profit of nearly 6 million rubles, which Hilferding calls "promoter's profits".

Our author puts the total "capacity" of the principal St. Petersburg banks at 8235 million rubles, well over 8 billion, and the "holdings", or rather, the extent to which foreign banks dominated them, he estimates as follows: French banks, 55%; British, 10%; German 35%. The author calculates that of the total of 8235 million rubles of functioning capital, 3687 million rubles, or over 40%, fall to the share of the Produgol and Prodamet syndicates* and the syndicates in the oil, metallurgical and cement industries. Thus, owing to the formation of capitalist monopolies, the merging of bank and industrial capital has also made enormous strides in Russia.

Finance capital, concentrated in a few hands and exercising a virtual monopoly, exacts enormous and ever-increasing profits from the floating of companies, issue of stock, state loans, etc., strengthens the domination of the financial oligarchy and levies tribute upon the whole of society for the benefit of monopolists. Here is an example, taken from a multitude of others, of the "business" methods of the American trusts, quoted by Hilferding. In 1887, Havemeyer founded the Sugar Trust by amalgamating 15 small firms, whose total capital amounted to 6.5 million dollars. Suitably "watered", as the Americans say, the capital of the trust was declared to be 50 million dollars. This "over-capitalisation" anticipated the monopoly profits, in the same way as the United States Steel Corporation anticipates its monopoly profits in buying up as many iron ore fields as possible. In fact, the Sugar Trust set up monopoly prices, which secured it such profits that it could pay 10% dividend on capital "watered" *sevenfold, or about 70% on the capital actually invested at the time the trust was formed!* In 1909, the capital of the Sugar Trust amounted to 90 million dollars. In 22 years, it had increased its capital more than tenfold.

In France the domination of the "financial oligarchy" (*Against the Financial Oligarchy in France*, the title of the well-known book by Lysis, the fifth edition of which was published in 1908) assumed a form that was only slightly different. Four of the most powerful banks enjoy, not a relative, but an "absolute monopoly" in the issue of bonds. In reality, this is a "trust of big banks". And monopoly ensures monopoly profits from bond issues. Usually a borrowing country does not get more than 90% of the sum of the loan, the remaining 10% goes to the banks and other middlemen. The profit made by the banks out of the Russo-Chinese loan of 400 million francs amounted to 8%; out of the Russian (1904) loan of 800 million francs the profit amounted to 10%; and out of the Moroccan (1904) loan of 62,500,000

---

* *Produgol*: an abbreviation for the Russian Society for Trade in Mineral Fuel of the Donets Basin. *Prodamet*: Society for Marketing Rusian Metallurgical Goods. — *Ed.*

francs it amounted to 18.75%. Capitalism, which began its development with petty usury capital, is ending its development with gigantic usury capital. "The French", says Lysis, "are the usurers of Europe." All the conditions of economic life are being profoundly modified by this transformation of capitalism. With a stationary population, and stagnant industry, commerce and shipping, the "country" can grow rich by usury. "Fifty persons, representing a capital of 8 million francs, can control *2000 million* francs deposited in four banks." The "holding system", with which we are already familiar, leads to the same result. One of the biggest banks, the Société Générale, for instance, issues 64,000 bonds for its "daughter company," the Egyptian Sugar Refineries. The bonds are issued at 150%, i.e., the bank gains 50 centimes on the franc. The dividends of the new company were found to be fictitious, the "public" lost from 90 to 100 million francs. "One of the directors of the Société Générale was a member of the board of directors of the Sugar Refineries." It is not surprising that the author is driven to the conclusion that "the French Republic is a financial monarchy"; "it is the complete domination of the financial oligarchy; the latter dominates over the press and the government."[53]

The extraordinary high rate of profit obtained from the issue of bonds, which is one of the principal functions of finance capital, plays a very important part in the development and consolidation of the financial oligarchy. "There is not a single business of this type within the country that brings in profits even approximately equal to those obtained from the flotation of foreign loans", says *Die Bank.*[54]

"No banking operation brings in profits comparable with those obtained from the issue of securities!" According to the *German Economist*, the average annual profits made on the issue of industrial stock were as follows:

	%
1895	38.6
1896	36.1
1897	66.7
1898	67.7
1899	66.9
1900	55.2

"In the ten years from 1891 to 1900 *more than a thousand million* marks were 'earned' by issuing German industrial stock."[55]

During periods of industrial boom, the profits of finance capital are immense, but during periods of depression, small and unsound businesses go out of existence and the big banks acquire "holdings" in them by buying them up for a mere song, or participate in profitable schemes for their "reconstruction" and "reorganisation". In the "reconstruction" of undertakings which have been running at a loss, "the share capital is written down, that is, profits are distributed on a smaller capital and continue to be calculated on this smaller basis. Or, if the income has fallen to zero, new capital is called in, which, combined with the old and less remunerative capital, will bring in an adequate return." "Incidentally," adds Hilferding, "all these reorganisations and reconstructions have a twofold significance for the banks: first, as profitable transactions; and secondly, as opportunities for securing control of the companies in difficulties."[56]

Here is an instance. The Union Mining Company of Dortmund was founded in 1872. Share capital was issued to the amount of nearly 40 million marks and the market price of the shares rose to 170 after it had paid a 12% dividend for its first year. Finance capital skimmed the cream and earned a trifle of something like 28 million marks. The principal sponsor of this company was that very big German Disconto-Gesellschaft which so successfully attained a capital of 300 million marks. Later, the dividends of the Union declined to nil: the shareholders had to consent to a "writing down" of capital, that is, to losing some of it in order not to lose it all. By a series of "reconstructions", more than 73 million marks were written off the books of the Union in the course of thirty years. "At the present time, the original shareholders of the company possess only 5% of the nominal value of their shares",[57] but the banks "earned something" out of every "reconstruction".

Speculation in land situated in the suburbs of rapidly growing big towns is a particularly profitable operation for finance capital. The monopoly of the banks merges here with the monopoly of ground-rent and with monopoly of the means of communication, since the rise in the price of land and the possibility of selling it profitably in lots, etc., is mainly dependent on good means of communication with the centre of the town; and these means of communication are in the hands of large companies which are connected with these same banks through the holding system and the distribution of seats on the boards. As a result we get what the German writer, L. Eschwege, a contributor to *Die Bank*, who has made a special study of real estate business and mortgages, etc., calls a "bog". Frantic speculation in suburban building lots; collapse of building enterprises like the Berlin firm of Boswau and Knauer, which acquired as much as 100 million marks with the help of the "sound and solid" Deutsche Bank - the latter, of course, acting through the holding system, i.e., secretly, behind the scenes — and got out of it with a loss of "only" 12 million marks, then the ruin of small proprietors and of workers who get nothing from the fictitious building firms, fraudulent deals with the "honest" Berlin police and administration for the purpose of gaining control of the issue of cadastral certificates, building licenses, etc., etc.[58]

"American ethics", which the European professors and well-meaning bourgeois so hypocritically deplore, have, in the age of finance capital, become the ethics of literally every large city in every country.

At the beginning of 1914, there was talk in Berlin of the formation of a "transport trust", i.e., of establishing "community of interests" between the three Berlin transport undertakings: the city electric railway, the tramway company and the omnibus company. "We have been aware", wrote *Die Bank*, "that this plan was contemplated since it became known that the majority of the shares in the bus company had been acquired by the other two transport companies... We may fully believe those who are pursuing this aim when they say that by uniting the transport services, they will secure economies, part of which will in time benefit the public. But the question is complicated by the fact that behind the transport trust that is being formed are the banks, which, if they desire, can subordinate the means of transportation, which they have monopolised, to the interests of their real estate business. To be convinced of the reasonableness of such a conjecture, we need only recall that the interests of the big bank that encouraged the formation of the Electric Railway Company were already involved in it at the time the company was formed. That is to say: the interests of this transport undertaking were interlocked with the real estate interests. The point is that the eastern line of this railway was to run across land which this bank sold at an enormous profit for itself and for several partners in the transactions when it became certain the line was to be laid down."[59]

A monopoly, once it is formed and controls thousands of millions, inevitably penetrates into *every* sphere of public life, regardless of the form of government and all other "details". In German economic literature one usually comes across obsequious praise of the integrity of the Prussian bureaucracy, and allusions to the French Panama scandal and to political corruption in America. But the fact is that *even* bourgeois literature devoted to German banking matters constantly has to go far beyond the field of purely banking operations; it speaks, for instance, about "the attraction of the banks" in reference to the increasing frequency with which public officials take employment with the banks, as follows: "How about the integrity of a state official who in his innermost heart is aspiring to a soft job in the Behrenstrasse?"[60] (the Berlin street where the head office of the Deutsche Bank is situated). In 1909, the publisher of *Die Bank*, Alfred Lansburgh, wrote an article entitled "The Economic Significance of Byzantinism", in which he incidentally referred to Wilhelm II's tour of Palestine, and to "the immediate result of this journey, the construction of the Baghdad railway, that fatal 'great product of German enterprise', which is more responsible for the 'encirclement' than all our political blunders put together".[61] (By encirclement is meant the policy of Edward VII to isolate Germany and surround her with an imperialist anti-German alliance.) In 1911, Eschwege, the contributor to this same magazine to whom I have already referred, wrote an article entitled "Plutocracy and Bureaucracy", in which he exposed, for example, the case of a German official named Völker, who was a zealous member of the Cartel Committee and who, it turned out some time later, obtained a lucrative post in the biggest cartel, i.e., the Steel Syndicate. Similar cases, by no means casual, forced this bourgeois author to admit that "the economic liberty guaranteed by the German Constitution has become in many departments of economic life, a meaningless phrase" and that under the existing rule of the plutocracy, "even the widest political liberty cannot save us from being converted into a nation of unfree people".[62]

As for Russia, I shall confine myself to one example. Some years ago, all the newspapers announced that Davydov, the director of the Credit Department of the Treasury, had resigned his post to take employment with a certain big bank at a salary which, according to the contract, would total over one million rubles in the course of several years. The Credit Department is an institution, the function of which is to "coordinate the activities of all the credit institutions of the country" and which grants subsidies to banks in St. Petersburg and Moscow amounting to between 800 and 1000 million rubles.[63]

It is characteristic of capitalism in general that the ownership of capital is separated from the application of capital to production, that money capital is separated from industrial or productive capital, and that the rentier who lives entirely on income obtained from money capital is separated from the entrepreneur and from all who are directly concerned in the management of capital. Imperialism, or the domination of finance capital, is that highest stage of capitalism at which this separation reaches vast proportions. The supremacy of finance capital over all other forms of capital means the predominance of the rentier and of the financial oligarchy; it means a small number of financially "powerful" states stand out among all the rest. The extent to which this process is going on may be judged from the statistics on emissions, i.e., the issue of all kinds of securities.

In the *Bulletin of the International Statistical Institute*, A. Neymarck[64] has published very comprehensive, complete and comparative figures covering the issue of securities all over the world, which have been repeatedly quoted in part in economic literature. The following are the totals he gives for four decades:

Total issues in francs per decade
(billions)

1871-1880 ....76.1
1881-1890 ....64.5
1891-1900 ....100.4
1901-1910 ....197.8

In the 1870s, the total amount of issues for the whole world was high, owing particularly to the loans floated in connection with the Franco-Prussian War, and the company-promotion boom which set in in Germany after the war. On the whole, the increase is relatively not very rapid during the three last decades of the 19th century, and only in the first ten years of the 20th century is an enormous increase of almost 100% to be observed. Thus the beginning of the 20th century marks the turning point, not only in the growth of monopolies (cartels, syndicates, trusts), of which we have already spoken, but also in the growth of finance capital.

Neymarck estimates the total amount of issued securities current in the world in 1910 at about 815,000 million francs. Deducting from this sum amounts which might have been duplicated, he reduces the total to 575-600 million, which is distributed among the various countries as follows (I take 600,000 million):

Financial securities current in 1910
(billion francs)

Great Britain............................ 142 ⎫	Holland 12.5
United States .... 132 ⎬ 479	Belgium 7.5
France...................................... 110 ⎪	Spain 7.5
Germany.................................... 95 ⎭	Switzerland 6.25
Russia.. 31	Denmark 3.75
Austria-Hungary 24	Sweden, Norway, Romania, etc. 2.5
Italy 14	
Japan 12	Total 600

From these figures we at once see standing out in sharp relief four of the richest capitalist countries, each of which holds securities to amounts ranging approximately from 100-150 billion francs. Of these four countries, two, Britain and France, are the oldest capitalist countries, and, as we shall see, possess the most colonies; the other two, the United States and Germany, are capitalist countries leading in the rapidity of development and the degree of extension of capitalist monopolies in industry. Together, these four countries own 479 billion francs, that is, nearly 80% of the world's finance capital. In one way or another, nearly the whole of the rest of the world is more or less the debtor to and tributary of these international banker countries, these four "pillars" of world finance capital.

It is particularly important to examine the part which the export of capital plays in creating the international network of dependence on and connections of finance capital. +

IV

EXPORT OF CAPITAL

TYPICAL OF THE OLD CAPITALISM, when free competition held undivided sway, was the export of *goods*. Typical of the latest stage of capitalism, when monopolies rule, is the export of *capital*.

Capitalism is commodity production at its highest stage of development, when labour-power itself becomes a commodity. The growth of internal exchange, and particularly of international exchange, is a characteristic feature of capitalism. The uneven and spasmodic development of individual enterprises, individual branches of industry and individual countries, is inevitable under the capitalist system. England became a capitalist country before any other, and by the middle of the 19th century, having adopted free trade, claimed to be the "workshop of the world," the supplier of manufactured goods to all countries, which in exchange were to keep her provided with raw materials. But in the last quarter of the 19th century, *this* monopoly was already undermined; for other countries, sheltering themselves with "protective" tariffs, developed into independent capitalist states. On the threshold of the 20th century we see the formation of a new type of monopoly: firstly, monopolist associations of capitalist in all capitalistically developed countries; secondly, the monopolist position of a few very rich countries, in which the accumulation of capital has reached gigantic proportions. An enormous "surplus of capital" has arisen in the advanced countries.

It goes without saying that if capitalism could develop agriculture, which today is everywhere lagging terribly behind industry, if it could raise the living standards of the masses, who in spite of the amazing technical progress are everywhere still half-starved and poverty-stricken, there could be no question of a surplus of capital. This "argument" is very often advanced by the petty-bourgeois critics of capitalism. But if capitalism did these things it would not be capitalism; for both uneven development and a semi-starvation level of existence of the masses are fundamental and inevitable conditions and constitute premises of this mode of production. As long as capitalism remains what it is, surplus capital will be utilised not for the purpose of raising the standard of living of the masses in a given country, for this would mean a decline in profits for the capitalists, but for the purpose of increasing profits by exporting capital abroad to the backward countries. In these backward countries profits are usually high, for capital is scarce, the price of land is relatively low, wages are low, raw materials are cheap. The export of capital is made possible by a number of backward countries having already been drawn into world capitalist intercourse; main railways have either been or are being built in those countries, elementary conditions for industrial development have been created, etc. The need to export capital arises from the fact that in a few countries capitalism has become "overripe" and (owing to the backward stage of agriculture and the poverty of the masses) capital cannot find a field for "profitable" investment.

Here are approximate figures showing the amount of capital invested abroad by the three principal countries:[65]

Capital invested abroad
(billion francs)

Year	Great Britain	France	Germany
1862	3.6	-	-
1872	15.0	10 (1869)	-
1882	22.0	15 (1880)	?
1893	42.0	20 (1890)	?
1902	62.0	27-37	12.5
1914	75-100.0	60	44.0

This table shows that the export of capital reached enormous dimensions only at the beginning of the 20th century. Before the war the capital invested abroad by the three principal countries amounted to between 175 billion and 200 billion francs. At the modest rate of 5%, the income from this sum should reach from 8-10 billion francs a year — a sound basis for imperialist oppression and the exploitation of most of the countries and nations of the world, for the capitalist parasitism of a handful of wealthy states!

How is this capital invested abroad distributed among the various countries? *Where* is it invested? Only an approximate answer can be given to these questions, but it is one sufficient to throw light on certain general relations and connections of modern imperialism.

Distribution (approximate) of foreign capital
in different parts of the globe (circa 1910)
(billion marks)

	Great Britain	France	Germany	Total
Europe	4	23	18	45
America	37	4	10	51
Asia, Africa and Australia	29	8	7	44
Total	70	35	35	140

The principal spheres of investment of British capital are the British colonies, which are very large also in America (for example, Canada), not to mention Asia, etc. In this case, enormous exports of capital are bound up most closely with vast colonies, of the importance of which for imperialism I shall speak later. In the case of France the situation is different. French capital exports are invested mainly in Europe, primarily in Russia (at least 10 billion francs). This is mainly *loan* capital, government loans and not capital invested in industrial undertakings. Unlike British colonial imperialism, French imperialism might be termed usury imperialism. In the case of Germany, we have a third type; colonies are inconsiderable, and German capital invested abroad is divided most evenly between Europe and America.

The export of capital influences and greatly accelerates the development of capitalism in those countries to which it is exported. While, therefore, the export of capital may tend to a certain extent to arrest development in the capital-exporting countries, it can only do so by expanding and deepening the further development of capitalism throughout the world.

The capital-exporting countries are nearly always able to obtain certain "advantages", the character of which throws light on the peculiarity of the epoch of finance capital and monopoly. The following passage, for instance, appeared in the Berlin review, *Die Bank*, for October 1913:

A comedy worthy of the pen of Aristophanes is lately being played on the international capital market. Numerous foreign countries, from Spain to the Balkan states, from Russia to Argentina, Brazil and China, are openly or secretly coming into the big money market with demands, sometimes very persistent, for loans. The money markets are not very bright at the moment and the political outlook is not promising. But not a single money market dares to refuse a loan for fear that its neighbour may forestall it, consent to grant a loan and so secure some reciprocal service. In these international transactions the creditor nearly always manages to secure some extra benefit: a favourable clause in a commercial treaty, a coaling station, a contract to construct a harbour, a fat concession, or an order for guns.[66]

Finance capital has created the epoch of monopolies, and monopolies introduce everywhere monopolist principles: the utilisation of "connections" for profitable transactions takes the place of competition on the open market. The most usual thing is to stipulate that part of the loan granted shall be spent on purchases in the creditor country, particularly on orders for war materials, or for ships, etc. In the course of the last two decades (1890-1910), France has very often resorted to this method. The export of capital thus becomes a means of encouraging the export of commodities. In this connection, transactions between particularly big firms assume a form which, as Schilder[67] "mildly" puts it, "borders on corruption". Krupp in Germany, Schneider in France, Armstrong in Britain are instances of firms which have close connections with powerful banks and governments and which cannot easily be "ignored" when a loan is being arranged.

France, when granting loans to Russia, "squeezed" her in the commercial treaty of September 16, 1905, stipulating for certain concessions to run till 1917. She did the same thing in the commercial treaty with Japan of August 19, 1911. The tariff war between Austria and Serbia, which lasted with a seven months' interval, from 1906 to 1911, was partly caused by Austria and France competing to supply Serbia with war materials. In January 1912, Paul Deschanel stated in the Chamber of Deputies that from 1908 to 1911 French firms had supplied war materials to Serbia to the value of 45 million francs.

A report from the Austro-Hungarian Consul at Sao-Paulo (Brazil) states: "The Brazilian railways are being built chiefly by French, Belgian, British and German capital. In the financial operations connected with the construction of these railways the countries involved stipulate for orders for the necessary railway materials."

Thus finance capital, literally, one might say, spreads its net over all countries of the world. An important role in this is played by banks founded in the colonies and by their branches. German imperialists look with envy at the "old" colonial countries which have been particularly "successful" in providing for themselves in this respect. In 1904 Great Britain had 50 colonial banks with 2279 branches (in 1910 there were 72 banks with 5449 branches), France had 20 with 136 branches; Holland, 16 with 68 branches; and Germany had "only" 13 with 70 branches.[68] The American capitalists, in their turn, are jealous of the English and German: "In South America", they complained in 1915, "five German banks have 40 branches and five English banks have 70 branches ... England and Germany have invested in Argentina, Brazil, and Uruguay in the last 25 years approximately four thousand million dollars, and as a result together enjoy 46% of the total trade of these three countries."[69]

The capital exporting countries have divided the world among themselves in the figurative sense of the term. But finance capital has led to the *actual* division of the world. +

V

DIVISION OF THE WORLD AMONG CAPITALIST ASSOCIATIONS

MONOPOLIST CAPITALIST ASSOCIATIONS, cartels, syndicates and trusts first divided the home market among themselves, and obtained more or less complete possession of the industry of their own country. But under capitalism the home market is inevitably bound up with the foreign market. Capitalism long ago created a world market. As the export of capital increased, and as the foreign and colonial connections and "spheres of influence" of the big monopolist associations expanded in all ways, things "naturally" gravitated towards an international agreement among these associations, and towards the formation of international cartels.

This is a new stage of world concentration of capital and production, incomparably higher than the preceding stages. Let us see how this supermonopoly develops.

The electrical industry is highly typical of the latest technical achievements, and is most typical of capitalism at the *end* of the 19th and the beginning of the 20th centuries. This industry has developed most in the two leaders of the new capitalist countries, the United States and Germany. In Germany, the crisis of 1900 gave a particularly strong impetus to its concentration. During the crisis, the banks, which by that time had become fairly well merged with industry, enormously accelerated and intensified the ruin of relatively small firms and their absorption by the large ones. "The banks", writes Jeidels, "refused a helping hand to the very firms in greatest need of capital, and brought on first a frenzied boom and then the hopeless failure of the companies which have not been connected with them closely enough."[70]

As a result, after 1900, concentration in Germany progressed with giant strides. Up to 1900 there had been seven or eight "groups" in the electrical industry. Each consisted of several companies (altogether there were 28) and each was backed by from two to 11 banks. Between 1908 and 1912 all these groups were merged into two, or one. The follwoing diagram shows the process:

Groups in the electrical industry

Prior to: 1900	Felten & Guillaume	Lahmeyer	Union. AEG	Siemens & Halske	Schuckert & Co.	Bergmann Kummer
	Felten & Lahmeyer		AEG (GEC)	Siemens & Halske -Schuckert		Bergmann Failed in 1900
By 1912:	AEG (GEC)			Siemens & Halske-Schuckert		

(In close "cooperation" since 1908)

The famous AEG (General Electric Company), which grew up in this way, controls 175 to 200 companies (through the "holding" system), and a total capital of approximately *1500 million* marks. Of direct agencies abroad alone, it has 34, of which 12 are joint-stock companies, in more than 10 countries. As early as 1904 the amount of capital invested abroad by the German electrical industry was estimated at 233 million marks. Of this sum, 62 million were invested in Russia. Needless to say, the AEG is a huge "combine" — its manufacturing companies alone number no less than 16 — producing the most diverse articles, from cables and insulators to motor cars and flying machines.

But concentration in Europe was also a component part of the process of concentration in America, which developed in the following way:

General Electric Company

United States:	Thomson-Houston Co. establishes a firm in Europe	Edison Co. establishes in Europe the French Edison Co. which transfers its patents to the German firm
Germany:	Union Electric Co.	General Electric Co. (AEG)

General Electric Co. (AEG)

Thus, *two* electrical "Great Powers" were formed: "there are no other electric companies in the world *completely* independent of them", wrote Heinig in his article "The Path of the Electric Trust". An idea, although far from complete, of the turnover and the size of the enterprises of the two "trusts" can be obtained from the following figures:

		Turnover (Mill. marks)	Number of employees	Net profits (Mill. marks)
America: General Electric Co. (GEC)	1907	252	28,000	35.4
	1910	298	32,000	45.6
Germany: General Electric Co. (AEG)	1907	216	30,700	14.5
	1911	362	60,800	21.7

And then, in 1907, the German and American trusts concluded an agreement by which they divided the world between themselves. Competition between them ceased. The American General Electric Company (GEC) "got" the United States and Canada. The German General Electric Company (AEG) "got" Germany, Austria, Russia, Holland, Denmark, Switzerland, Turkey and the Balkans. Special agreements, naturally secret, were concluded regarding the penetration of "daughter companies" into new branches of industry, into "new" countries formally not yet allotted. The two trusts were to exchange inventions and experiments.[71]

The difficulty of competing against this trust, actually a single world-wide trust controlling a capital of several billion, with "branches", agencies, representatives, connections, etc., in every corner of the world, is self-evident. But the division of the world between two powerful trusts does not preclude *redivision* if the relation of forces changes as a result of uneven development, war, bankruptcy, etc.

An instructive example of an attempt at such a redivision, of the struggle for redivision, is provided by the oil industry.

"The world oil market", wrote Jeidels in 1905, "is even today still divided between two great financial groups — Rockefeller's American Standard Oil Co., and Rothschild and Nobel, the controlling interests of the Russian oilfields in Baku. The two groups are closely connected. But for several years five enemies have been threatening their monopoly":[72] (1) The exhaustion of the American oilfields; (2) the competition of the firm of Mantashev of Baku; (3) the Austrian oilfields; (4) the Romanian oilfields; (5) the overseas oilfields, particularly in the Dutch colonies (the extremely rich firms, Samuel, and Shell, also connected with British capital). The three last groups are connected with the big German banks, headed by the huge Deutsche Bank. These banks independently and systematically developed the oil industry in Romania, for example, in order to have a foothold of their "own." In 1907, the foreign capital invested in the Romanian oil industry was estimated at 185 million francs, of which 74 million was German capital.[73]

A struggle began for the "division of the world", as, in fact, it is called in economic literature. On the one hand, the Rockefeller "oil trust", wanted to lay its hands on *everything*, it formed a "daughter company" *right* in Holland, and bought up oilfields in the Dutch Indies, in order to strike at its principal enemy, the Anglo-Dutch Shell trust. On the other hand, the Deutsche Bank and the other German banks aimed at "retaining" Romania "for themselves" and at uniting her with Russia against Rockefeller. The latter possessed far more capital and an excellent system of oil transportation and distribution. The struggle had to end, and did end in 1907, with the utter defeat of the Deutsche Bank, which was confronted with the alternative: either to liquidate its "oil interests" and lose millions, or submit. It chose to submit, and concluded a very disadvantageous agreement with the "oil trust". The Deutsche Bank agreed "not to attempt anything which might injure American interests". Provision was made however, for the annulment of the agreement in the event of Germany establishing a state oil monopoly.

Then the "comedy of oil" began. One of the German finance kings, von Gwinner, a director of the Deutsche Bank through his private secretary, Stauss, launched a campaign *for* a state oil monopoly. The gigantic machine of the huge German bank and all its wide "connections" were set in motion. The press bubbled over with "patriotic" indignation against the "yoke" of the American trust, and, on March 15, 1911 the Reichstag by an almost unanimous vote, adopted a motion asking the government to introduce a bill for the establishment of an oil monopoly. The government seized upon this "popular" idea, and the game of the Deutsche Bank, which hoped to cheat its American counterpart and improve its business by a state monopoly, appeared to have been won. The German oil magnates already saw visions of enormous profits, which would not be less than those of the Russian sugar refiners ... But, firstly, the big German banks quarrelled among themselves over the division of the spoils. The Disconto-Gesellschaft exposed the covetous aims of the Deutsche Bank; secondly, the government took fright at the prospect of a struggle with Rockefeller, for it was very doubtful whether Germany could be sure of obtaining oil from other sources (the Romanian output was small); thirdly, just at that time the 1913 credits of a billion marks were voted for Germany's war preparations. The oil monopoly project was postponed. The Rockefeller "oil trust" came out of the struggle, for the time being, victorious.

The Berlin review, *Die Bank*, wrote in this connection that Germany could fight the oil trust only by establishing an electricity monopoly and by converting water-power into cheap electricity. "But", the author added, "the electricity monopoly will come when the producers need it, that is to say when the next great crash in the electrical industry is imminent, and when the gigantic, expensive power stations now being put up at great cost everywhere by private electrical 'concerns', which are already obtaining certain franchises from towns, from states, etc., can no longer work at a profit. Water-power will then have to be used. But it will be impossible to convert it into cheap electricity at state expense; it will also have to be handed over to a 'private monopoly controlled by the state', because private industry has already concluded a number of contracts and has stipulated for heavy compensation ... So it was with the nitrate monopoly, so it is with the oil monopoly; so it will be with the electric power monopoly. It is time our state socialists, who allow themselves to be blinded by a beautiful principle, understood, at last, that in Germany the monopolies have never pursued the aim, nor have they had the result, of benefiting the consumer, or even of handing over to the state part of the promoter's profits; they have served only to facilitate at the expense of the state, the recovery of private industries which were on the verge of bankruptcy."[74]

Such are the valuable admissions which the German bourgeois economists are forced to make. We see plainly here how private and state monopolies are interwoven in the age of finance capital; how both are but separate links in the imperialist struggle between the big monopolists for the division of the world.

In merchant shipping, the tremendous development of concentration has ended also in the division of the world. In Germany two powerful companies have come to the fore: the Hamburg-Amerika and the Norddeutscher Lloyd, each having a capital of 200 million marks (in stocks and bonds) and possessing shipping tonnage to the value of 185 to 189 million marks. On the other hand, in America, on January 1, 1903, the International Mercantile Marine Co., known as the Morgan trust, was formed; it united nine American and British steamship companies, and which possessed a capital of 120 million dollars (480 million marks). As early as 1903, the German giants and this American-British trust concluded an agreement to divide the world with a consequent division of profits. The German companies undertook not to compete in the Anglo-American traffic. Which ports were to be "allotted" to each was precisely stipulated; a joint committee of control was set up, etc. This agreement was concluded for 20 years, with the prudent provision for its annulment in the event of war.[75]

Extremely instructive also is the story of the formation of the International Rail Cartel. The first attempt of the British, Belgian and German rail manufacturers to form such a cartel was made as early as 1884, during a severe industrial depression. The manufacturers agreed not to compete with one another in the home markets of the countries involved, and they divided the foreign markets in the following quotas: Great Britain 66%; Germany 27%; Belgium 7%. India was reserved entirely for Great Britain. Joint war was declared against a British firm which remained outside the cartel, the cost of which was met by a percentage levy on all sales. But in 1886 the cartel collapsed when two British firms retired from it. It is characteristic that agreement could not be achieved during subsequent boom periods. At the beginning of 1904, the German steel syndicate was formed. In November 1904, the International Rail Cartel was revived, with the following quotas: Britain 53.5%; Germany 28.83%; Belgium 17.67%. France came in later and received 4.8%, 5.8% and 6.4% in the first, second and third years respectively, over and above the 100% limit, i.e., out of a total of 104.8%, etc. In 1905, the United States Steel Corporation entered the cartel; then Austria and Spain. "At the present time", wrote Vogelstein in 1910, "the division of the world is complete, and the big consumers, primarily the state railways — since the world has been parceled out without consideration for their interests — can now dwell like the poet in the heaven of Jupiter."[76]

Let me also mention the International Zinc Syndicate which was established in 1909 and which precisely apportioned output among five groups of factories: German, Belgian, French, Spanish and British; and also the International Dynamite Trust, which, Liefmann says, is "quite a modern, close alliance of all the German explosives manufacturers who, with the French and American dynamite manufacturers, organised in a similar manner, have divided the whole world among themselves, so to speak".[77]

Liefmann calculated that in 1897 there were altogether about 40 international cartels in which Germany had a share, while in 1910 there were about a hundred.

Certain bourgeois writers (now joined by Karl Kautsky, who has completely abandoned the Marxist position he held, for example, in 1909) have expressed the opinion that international cartels, being one of the most striking expressions of the internationalisation of capital, give the hope of peace among nations under capitalism. Theoretically, this opinion is absolutely absurd, while in practice it is sophistry and a dishonest defense of the worst opportunism. International cartels show to what point capitalist monopolies have developed, and *the object* of the struggle between the various capitalist associations. This last circumstance is the most important, it alone shows us the historico-economic meaning of what is taking place; for the *forms* of the struggle may and do constantly change in accordance with varying, relatively specific and temporary causes, but the *substance* of the struggle, its class *content*, positively *cannot* change while classes exist. Naturally, it is in the interests of, for example, the German bourgeoisie, to whose side Kautsky has in effect gone over in his theoretical arguments (I shall deal with this later), to obscure the *substance* of the present economic struggle (the division of the world) and to emphasise now this and now another *form* of the struggle. Kautsky makes the same mistake. Of course, we have in mind not only the German bourgeoisie, but the bourgeoisie all over the world. The capitalists divide the world, not out of any particular malice, but because the degree of concentration which has been reached forces them to adopt this method in order to obtain profits. And they divide it "in proportion to capital", "in proportion to strength", because there cannot be any other method of division under commodity production and capitalism. But strength varies with the degree of economic and political development. In order to understand what is taking place, it is necessary to know what questions are settled by the changes in strength. The question as to whether these changes are "purely" economic or *non*-economic (e.g., military) is a secondary one, which cannot in the least affect fundamental views on the latest epoch of capitalism. To substitute the question of the form of the struggle and agreements (today peaceful, tomorrow warlike, the next day warlike again) for the question of the *substance* of the struggle and agreements between capitalist associations is to sink to the role of a sophist.

The epoch of the latest stage of capitalism shows us that certain relations between capitalist associations grow up, *based* on the economic division of the world, while parallel to and in connection with it, certain relations grow up between political alliances, between states, on the basis of the territorial division of the world, of the struggle for colonies, of the "struggle for spheres of influence". +

VI

DIVISION OF THE WORLD AMONG THE GREAT POWERS

IN HIS BOOK on "the territorial development of the European colonies", A. Supan,[78] the geographer, gives the following brief summary of this development at the end of the nineteenth century:

Percentage of territory belonging to the European colonial powers
(including the United States)

	1876	1900	Increase or decrease
Africa	10.8	90.4	+ 79.6
Polynesia	56.8	98.9	+ 42.1
Asia	51.5	56.6	+ 5.1
Australia	100.0	100.0	-
America	27.5	27.2	-0.3

"The characteristic feature of this period", he concludes, "is, therefore, the division of Africa and Polynesia." As there are no unoccupied territories — that is, territories that do not belong to any state — in Asia and America, it is necessary to amplify Supan's conclusion and say that the characteristic feature of the period under review is the final partitioning of the globe — final, not in the sense that a *repartition* is impossible; on the contrary, repartitions are possible and inevitable — but in the sense that the colonial policy of the capitalist countries has *completed* the seizure of the unoccupied territories on our planet. For the first time the world is completely divided up, so that in the future *only* redivision is possible, i.e., territories can only pass from one "owner" to another, instead of passing as ownerless territory to an "owner".

Hence, we are living in a peculiar epoch of world colonial policy, which is most closely connected with the "latest stage in the development of capitalism", with finance capital. For this reason, it is essential first of all to deal in greater detail with the facts, in order to ascertain as exactly as possible what distinguishes this epoch from those preceding it, and what the present situation is. In the first place, two questions of fact arise here: is an intensification of colonial policy, a sharpening of the struggle for colonies, observed precisely in the epoch of finance capital? And how, in this respect, is the world divided at the present time?

The American writer, Morris, in his book on the history of colonisation,[79] made an attempt to sum up the data on the colonial possessions of Great Britain, France and Germany during different periods of the 19th century. The following is a brief summary of the results he has obtained:

Colonial possessions

	Great Britain		France		Germany	
Year (mill.)	Area (mill. sq.m.)	Pop. (mill.)	Area (mill. sq.m.)	Pop. (mill.)	Area (mill. sq.m.)	Pop.
1815-30	?	126.4	0.02	0.5	-	-
1860	2.5	145.1	0.2	3.4	-	-
1880	7.7	267.9	0.7	7.5	-	-
1899	9.3	309.0	3.7	56.4	1.0	14.7

For Great Britain, the period of the enormous expansion of colonial conquests was that between 1860 and 1880, and it was also very considerable in the last 20 years of the 19th century. For France and Germany this period falls precisely in these 20 years. We saw above that the development of premonopoly capitalism, of capitalism in which free competition was predominant, reached its limit in the 1860s and 1870s. We now see that it is *precisely after that period* that the tremendous "boom" in colonial conquests begins, and that the struggle for the territorial division of the world becomes extraordinarily sharp. It is beyond doubt, therefore, that capitalism's transition to the stage of monopoly capitalism, to finance capital, *is connected* with the intensification of the struggle for the partitioning of the world.

Hobson, in his work on imperialism, marks the years 1884-1900 as the epoch of intensified "expansion" of the chief European states. According to his estimate, Great Britain during these years acquired 3,700,000 square miles of territory with 57 million inhabitants; France 3,600,000 square miles with 36.5 million; Germany one million square miles with 14.7 million; Belgium 900,000 square miles with 30 million; Portugal 800,000 square miles with 9 million. The scramble for colonies by all the capitalist states at the end of the 19th century and particularly since the 1880s is a commonly known fact in the history of diplomacy and of foreign policy.

In the most flourishing period of free competition in Great Britain, i.e., between 1840 and 1860, the leading British bourgeois politicians were *opposed* to colonial policy and were of the opinion that the liberation of the colonies, their complete separation from Britain, was inevitable and desirable. M. Beer, in an article, "Modern British Imperialism",[80] published in 1898, shows that in 1852, Disraeli, a statesman who was generally inclined towards imperialism, declared: "The colonies are millstones round our necks." But at the end of the 19th century the British heroes of the hour were Cecil Rhodes and Joseph Chamberlain, who openly advocated imperialism and applied the imperialist policy in the most cynical manner!

It is not without interest to observe that even then these leading British bourgeois politicians saw the connection between what might be called the purely economic and the socio-political roots of modern imperialism. Chamberlain advocated imperialism as a "true, wise and economical policy", and pointed particularly to the German, American and Belgian competition which Great Britain was encountering in the world market. Salvation lies in monopolies, said the capitalists as they formed cartels, syndicates and trusts. Salvation lies in monopoly, echoed the political leaders of the bourgeoisie, hastening to appropriate the parts of the world not yet shared out. And Cecil Rhodes, we are informed by his intimate friend, the journalist Stead, expressed his imperialist views to him in 1895 in the following terms: "I was in the East End of London [a working-class quarter] yesterday and attended a meeting of the unemployed. I listened to the wild speeches, which were just a cry for 'bread,' 'bread!' and on my way home I pondered over the scene and I became more than ever convinced of the importance of imperialism ... My cherished idea is a solution for the social problem, i.e., in order to save the 40 million inhabitants of the United Kingdom from a bloody civil war, we colonial statesmen must acquire new lands to settle the surplus population, to provide new markets for the goods produced in the factories and mines. The Empire, as I have always said, is a bread and butter question. If you want to avoid civil war, you must become imperialists."[81]

Thas was said in 1895 by Cecil Rhodes, millionaire, a king of finance, the man who was mainly responsible for the Anglo-Boer War. True, his defence of imperialism is crude and cynical, but in substance it does not differ from the "theory" advocated by Messrs. Maslov, Südekum, Potresov, David, the founder of Russian Marxism, and others. Cecil Rhodes was a somewhat more honest social-chauvinist ...

To present as precise a picture as possible of the territorial division of the world and of the changes which have occurred during the last decades in this respect, I shall utilise the data furnished by Supan in the work already quoted on the colonial possessions of all the powers of the world. Supan takes the years 1876 and 1900; I shall take the year 1876 — a year very aptly selected, for it is precisely by that time that the pre-monopolist stage of development of West-European capitalism can be said to have been, in the main, completed — and the year 1914, and instead of Supan's figures I shall quote the more recent statistics of Hübner's *Geographical and Statistical Tables*. Supan gives figures only for colonies; I think it useful, in order to present a complete picture of the division of the world, to add brief data on non-colonial and semi-colonial countries, in which category I place Persia, China and Turkey: the first of these countries is already almost completely a colony, the second and third are becoming such.

We thus get the following result:

Colonial possessions of the Great Powers
(Million square kilometres and million inhabitants)

	Colonies				Metropolitan countries		Total	
	1876		*1914*		*1914*		*1914*	
	Area	Pop.	Area	Pop.	Area	Pop.	Area	Pop.
Great Britain	22.5	251.9	33.5	393.5	0.3	46.5	33.8	440.0
Russia	17.0	15.9	17.4	33.2	5.4	136.2	22.8	169.4
France	0.9	6.0	10.6	55.5	0.5	39.6	11.1	95.1
Germany	-	-	2.9	12.3	0.5	64.9	3.4	77.2
U.S.A.	-	-	0.3	9.7	9.4	97.0	9.7	106.7
Japan	-	-	0.3	19.2	0.4	53.0	0.7	72.2
Total for 6 Great Powers	40.4	273.8	65.0	523.4	16.5	437.2	81.5	960.6
Colonies of other powers (Belgium, Holland, etc.)							9.9	45.3
Semi-colonial countries (Persia, China, Turkey)							14.5	361.2
Other countries							28.0	289.9
Total for whole world							133.9	1657.0

We clearly see from these figures how "complete" was the partition of the world at the turn of the 20th century. After 1876 colonial possessions increased to enormous dimensions, more than 50%, from 40 million to 65 million square kilometers for the six biggest powers; the increase amounts to 25 million square kilometers, 50% larger than the area of the metropolitan countries (16,500,000 square kilometres). In 1876 three powers had no colonies, and a fourth, France, had scarcely any. By 1914 these four powers had acquired colonies of an area of 14,100,000 square kilometres, i.e., about half as much again as the area of Europe, with a population of nearly 100 million. The unevenness in the rate of expansion of colonial possessions is very great. If, for instance, we compare France, Germany and Japan, which do not differ very much in area and population, we will see that the first has acquired almost three times as much colonial territory as the other two combined. In regard to finance capital, France, at the beginning of the period we are considering, was also, perhaps, several times richer than Germany and Japan put together. In addition to, and on the basis of, purely economic conditions, geographical and other conditions also affect the dimensions of colonial possessions. However strong the process of levelling the world, of leveling the economic and living conditions in different countries, may have been in the past decades as a result of the pressure of large-scale industry, exchange and finance capital, considerable differences still remain; and among the six countries mentioned we see, firstly, young capitalist countries (America, Germany, Japan) whose progress has been extraordinarily rapid; secondly, countries with an old capitalist development (France and Great Britain), whose progress lately has been much slower than that of the previously mentioned countries, and thirdly, a country most backward economically (Russia), where modern capitalist imperialism is enmeshed, so to speak, in a particularly close network of pre-capitalist relations.

Alongside the colonial possessions of the Great Powers, we have placed the small colonies of the small states, which are, so to speak, the next objects of a possible and probable "redivision" of colonies. These small states mostly retain their colonies only because the big powers are torn by conflicting interests, friction, etc., which prevent them from coming to an agreement on the division of the spoils. As to the "semicolonial" states, they provide an example of the transitional forms which are to be found in all spheres of nature and society. Finance capital is such a great, such a decisive, you might say, force in all economic and in all international relations, that it is capable of subjecting, and actually does subject to itself even states enjoying the fullest political independence; we shall shortly see examples of this. Of course, finance capital finds most "convenient", and derives the greatest profit from, a *form* of subjection which involves the loss of the political independence of the subjected countries and peoples. In this respect, the semicolonial countries provide a typical example of the "middle stage". It is natural that the struggle for these semi-dependent countries should have become particularly bitter in the epoch of finance capital, when the rest of the world has already been divided up.

Colonial policy and imperialism existed before the latest stage of capitalism, and even before capitalism. Rome, founded on slavery, pursued a colonial policy and practiced imperialism. But "general" disquisitions on imperialism, which ignore, or put into the background, the fundamental difference between socio-economic systems, inevitably turn into the most vapid banality or bragging, like the comparison: "Greater

Rome and Greater Britain".[82] Even the capitalist colonial policy of *previous* stages of capitalism is essentially different from the colonial policy of finance capital.

The principal feature of the latest stage of capitalism is the domination of monopolist associations of the big employers. These monopolies are most firmly established when *all* the sources of raw materials are captured by one group, and we have seen with what zeal the international capitalist associations exert every effort to deprive their rivals of all opportunity of competing, to buy up, for example, ironfields, oilfields, etc. Colonial possession alone gives the monopolies complete guarantee against all contingencies in the struggle against competitors, including the case of the adversary wanting to be protected by a law establishing a state monopoly. The more capitalism is developed, the more strongly the shortage of raw materials is felt, the more intense the competition and the hunt for sources of raw materials throughout the whole world, the more desperate the struggle for the acquisition of colonies.

"It may be asserted", writes Schilder, "although it may sound paradoxical to some, that in the more or less foreseeable future the growth of the urban and industrial population is more likely to be hindered by a shortage of raw materials for industry than by a shortage of food." For example, there is a growing shortage of timber — the price of which is steadily rising — of leather, and of raw materials for the textile industry. "Associations of manufacturers are making efforts to create an equilibrium between agriculture and industry in the whole of world economy; as an example of this we might mention the International Federation of Cotton Spinners' Associations in several of the most important industrial countries, founded in 1904, and the European Federation of Flax Spinners' Associations, founded on the same model in 1910."[83]

Of course, the bourgeois reformists, and among them particularly the present-day adherents of Kautsky, try to belittle the importance of facts of this kind by arguing that raw materials "could be" obtained in the open market without a "costly and dangerous" colonial policy; and that the supply of raw materials "could be" increased enormously by "simply" improving conditions in agriculture in general. But such arguments become an apology for imperialism, an attempt to paint it in bright colours, because they ignore the principal feature of the latest stage of capitalism: monopolies. The free market is becoming more and more a thing of the past; monopolist syndicates and trusts are restricting it with every passing day, and "simply" improving conditions in agriculture means improving the conditions of the masses, raising wages and reducing profits. Where, except in the imagination of sentimental reformists, are there any trusts capable of concerning themselves with the condition of the masses instead of the conquest of colonies?

Finance capital is interested not only in the already discovered sources of raw materials but also in potential sources, because present-day technical development is extremely rapid, and land which is useless today may be improved tomorrow if new methods are devised (to this end a big bank can equip a special expedition of engineers, agricultural experts, etc.), and if large amounts of capital are invested. This also applies to prospecting for minerals, to new methods of processing up and utilising raw materials, etc., etc. Hence, the inevitable striving of finance capital to enlarge its spheres of influence and even its actual territory. In the same way that the trusts capitalise their property at two or three times its value, taking into account its "potential" (and not actual) profits, and the further results of monopoly, so finance capital in general strives to seize the largest possible amount of land of all kinds in all places, and by every means, taking into account potential sources of raw materials and fearing to be left behind in the fierce struggle for the last remnants of independent territory, or for the repartition of those territories that have been already divided.

The British capitalists are exerting every effort to develop cotton growing in *their* colony, Egypt (in 1904, out of 2,300,000 hectares of land under cultivation, 600,000, or more than one-fourth, were under cotton); the Russians are doing the same in *their* colony, Turkestan, because in this way they will be in a better position to defeat their foreign competitors, to monopolise the sources of raw materials and form a more economical and profitable textile trust in which *all* the processes of cotton production and manufacturing will be "combined" and concentrated in the hands of one set of owners.

The interests pursued in exporting capital also give an impetus to the conquest of colonies, for in the colonial market it is easier to employ monopoly methods (and sometimes they are the only methods that can be employed) to eliminate competition, to ensure supplies, to secure the necessary "connections," etc.

The non-economic superstructure which grows up on the basis of finance capital, its politics and its ideology, stimulates the striving for colonial conquest. "Finance capital does not want liberty, it wants domination", as Hilferding very truly says. And a French bourgeois writer, developing and supplementing, as it were, the ideas of Cecil Rhodes quoted above, writes that social causes should be added to the economic causes of modern colonial policy:

> Owing to the growing complexities of life and the difficulties which weigh not only on the masses of the workers, but also on the middle classes, "impatience, irritation and hatred are accumulating in all the countries of the old civilisation and are becoming a menace to public order; the energy which is being hurled out of the definite class channel

must be given employment abroad in order to avert an explosion at home".[84]

Since we are speaking of colonial policy in the epoch of capitalist imperialism, it must be observed that finance capital and its foreign policy, which is the struggle of the great powers for the economic and political division of the world, give rise to a number of *transitional* forms of state dependence. Not only are the two main groups of countries, those owning colonies, and the colonies themselves, but also the diverse forms of dependent countries which, politically, are formally independent, but in fact, are enmeshed in the net of financial and diplomatic dependence typical of this epoch. We have already referred to one form of dependence — the semi-colony. An example of another is provided by Argentina.

"South America, and especially Argentina", writes Schulze-Gaevernitz in his work on British imperialism, "is so dependent financially on London that it ought to be described as almost a British commercial colony."[85] Basing himself on the report of the Austro-Hungarian consul at Buenos Aires for 1909, Schilder estimates the amount of British capital invested in Argentina at 8,750,000 francs. It is not difficult to imagine what strong connections British finance capital (and its faithful "friend", diplomacy) thereby acquires with the Argentine bourgeoisie, with the circles that control the whole of that country's economic and political life.

A somewhat different form of financial and diplomatic dependence, accompanied by political independence, is presented by Portugal. Portugal is an independent sovereign state, but actually, for more than 200 years, since the war of the Spanish Succession (1701-14), it has been a British protectorate. Great Britain has protected Portugal and her colonies in order to fortify her own positions in the fight against her rivals, Spain and France. In return Great Britain has received commercial privileges, preferential conditions for importing goods and especially capital into Portugal and the Portuguese colonies, the right to use the ports and islands of Portugal, her telegraph cables, etc.[86] Relations of this kind have always existed between big and little states, but in the epoch of capitalist imperialism they become a general system, they form part of the sum total of "divide the world" relations and become links in the chain of operations of world finance capital.

In order to finish with the question of the division of the world, I must make the following additional observation. This question was raised quite openly and definitely not only in American literature after the Spanish-American War, and in English literature after the Anglo-Boer War, at the very end of the 19th century and the beginning of the 20th; not only has German literature, which has "most jealously" watched "British imperialism", systematically given its appraisal of this fact. This question has also been raised in French bourgeois literature as definitely and broadly as is thinkable from the bourgeois point of view. Let me quote Driault, the historian, who, in his book, *Political and Social Problems at the End of the Nineteenth Century*, in the chapter "The Great Powers and the Division of the World", wrote the following:

During the past few years, all the free territory of the globe, with the exception of China, has been occupied by the powers of Europe and North America. This has already brought about several conflicts and shifts of spheres of influence, and those foreshadow more terrible upheavals in the near future. For it is necessary to make haste. The nations which have not yet made provision for themselves run the risk of never receiving their share and never participating in the tremendous exploitation of the globe which will be one of the most essential features of the next century [i.e., the 20th] ... That is why all Europe and America have lately been afflicted with the fever of colonial expansion, of "imperialism," that most noteworthy feature of the end of the nineteenth century." [And the author added:] In this partition of the world, in this furious hunt for the treasures and the big markets of the globe, the relative strength of the empires founded in this nineteenth century is totally out of proportion to the place occupied in Europe by the nations which founded them. The dominant powers in Europe, the arbiters of her destiny, are *not* equally preponderant in the whole world. And, as colonial might, the hope of controlling as yet unassessed wealth, will evidently react upon the relative strength of the European powers, the colonial question — "imperialism" if you will — which has already modified the political conditions of Europe itself, will modify them more and more.[87] +

VII

IMPERIALISM, AS A SPECIAL STAGE OF CAPITALISM

WE MUST NOW TRY to sum up, to draw together the threads of what has been said above on the subject of imperialism. Imperialism emerged as the development and direct continuation of the fundamental characteristics of capitalism in general. But capitalism only became capitalist imperialism at a definite and very high stage of its development, when certain of its fundamental characteristics began to change into their opposites, when the features of the epoch of transition from capitalism to a higher social and economic system had taken shape and revealed themselves in all spheres. Economically, the main thing in this process is the displacement of capitalist free competition by capitalist monopoly. Free competition is the basic feature of capitalism, and of commodity production generally; monopoly is the exact opposite of free competition, but we have seen the latter being transformed into monopoly before our eyes, creating large-scale industry and forcing out small industry, replacing large-scale by still larger-scale industry, and carrying concentration of production and capital to the point where out of it has grown and is growing monopoly: cartels, syndicates and trusts, and merging with them, the capital of a dozen or so banks, which manipulate thousands of millions. At the same time the monopolies, which have grown out of free competition, do not eliminate the latter, but exist above it and alongside it, and thereby give rise to a number of very acute, intense antagonisms, frictions and conflicts. Monopoly is the transition from capitalism to a higher system.

If it were necessary to give the briefest possible definition of imperialism we should have to say that imperialism is the monopoly stage of capitalism. Such a definition would include what is most important, for, on the one hand, finance capital is the bank capital of a few very big monopolist banks, merged with the capital of the monopolist associations of industrialists; and, on the other hand, the division of the world is the transition from a colonial policy which has extended without hindrance to territories unseized by any capitalist power, to a colonial policy of monopolist possession of the territory of the world which has been completely divided up.

But very brief definitions, although convenient, for they sum up the main points, are nevertheless inadequate, since we have to deduce from them some especially important features of the phenomenon that has to be defined. And so, without forgetting the conditional and relative value of all definitions in general, which can never embrace all the concatenations of a phenomenon in its full development, we must give a definition of imperialism that will include the following five of its basic features: (1) the concentration of production and capital has developed to such a high stage that it has created monopolies which play a decisive role in economic life; (2) the merging of bank capital with industrial capital, and the creation, on the basis of this "finance capital", of a financial oligarchy; (3) the export of capital as distinguished from the export of commodities acquires exceptional importance; (4) the formation of international monopolist capitalist associations which share the world among themselves, and (5) the territorial division of the whole world among the biggest capitalist powers is completed. Imperialism is capitalism in that stage of development at which the dominance of monopolies and finance capital is established; in which the export of capital has acquired pronounced importance; in which the division of the world among the international trusts has begun; in which the division of all territories of the globe among the biggest capitalist powers has been completed.

We shall see later that imperialism can and must be defined differently if we bear in mind, not only the basic, purely economic concepts — to which the above definition is limited — but also the historical place of this stage of capitalism in relation to capitalism in general, or the relation between imperialism and the two main trends in the working-class movement. The thing to be noted just at this point is that imperialism, as interpreted above, undoubtedly represents a special stage in the development of capitalism. To enable the reader to obtain the most well-grounded idea of imperialism possible, I deliberately tried to quote as extensively as possible *bourgeois* economists who have to admit the particularly incontrovertible facts concerning the latest stage of capitalist economy. With the same object in view, I have quoted detailed statistics which enable one to see to what degree bank capital, etc., has grown, in what precisely the transformation of quantity into quality, of developed capitalism into imperialism, was expressed. Needless to say, of course, all boundaries in nature and in society are conventional and changeable, that it would be absurd to argue, for example, about the particular year or decade in which imperialism "definitely" became established.

In the matter of defining imperialism, however, we have to enter into controversy, primarily, with Karl Kautsky, the principal Marxian theoretician of the epoch of the so-called Second International — that is, of the 25 years between 1889 and 1914. The fundamental ideas expressed in our definition of imperialism were very resolutely attacked by Kautsky in 1915, and even in November 1914, when he said that imperialism must not be regarded as a "phase" or stage of economy, but as a policy, a definite policy "preferred" by finance capital; that imperialism must not be "identified" with "present-day capitalism"; that if imperialism is to be understood to mean "all the phenomena of present-day capitalism" — cartels, protection, the domination of the financiers, and colonial policy — then the question as to whether imperialism is necessary to capitalism becomes reduced to the "flattest tautology", because, in that case, "imperialism is naturally a vital necessity for capitalism", and so on. The best way to present Kautsky's idea is to quote his own definition of imperialism, which is diametrically opposed to the substance of the ideas which I have set forth (for the objections coming from the camp of the German Marxists, who have been advocating similar ideas for many years already, have been long known to Kautsky as the objections of a definite trend in Marxism).

Kautsky's definition is as follows:

> Imperialism is a product of highly developed industrial capitalism. It consists in the striving of every industrial capitalist nation to bring under its control or to annex all large areas of *agrarian* [Kautsky's italics] territory, irrespective of what nations inhabit it.[88]

This definition is of no use at all because it one-sidedly, i.e., arbitrarily, singles out only the national question (although the latter is extremely important in itself as well as in its relation to imperialism), it arbitrarily and *inaccurately* connects this question *only* with industrial capital in the countries which annex other nations, and in an equally arbitrary and inaccurate manner pushes into the forefront the annexation of agrarian regions.

Imperialism is a striving for annexations — this is what the *political* part of Kautsky's definition amounts to. It is correct, but very incomplete, for politically, imperialism is, in general, a striving towards violence and reaction. For the moment, however, we are interested in the *economic* aspect of the question, which Kautsky *himself* introduced into *his* definition. The inaccuracies in Kautsky's definition are glaring. The characteristic feature of imperialism is *not* industrial *but* finance capital. It is not an accident that in France it was precisely the extraordinarily rapid development of *finance* capital, and the weakening of industrial capital, that, from the [18]80s onwards, gave rise to the extreme intensification of annexationist (colonial) policy.

The characteristic feature of imperialism is precisely that it strives to annex *not only* agrarian territories, but even most highly industrialised regions (German appetite for Belgium; French appetite for Lorraine), because (1) the fact that the world is already partitioned obliges those contemplating a *redivision* to reach out for *every kind* of territory, and (2) an essential feature of imperialism is the rivalry between several great powers in the striving for hegemony, i.e., for the conquest of territory, not so much directly for themselves as to weaken the adversary and undermine *his* hegemony. (Belgium is particularly important for Germany as a base for operations against Britain; Britain needs Baghdad as a base for operations against Germany, etc.)

Kautsky refers especially — and repeatedly — to English writers who, he alleges, have given a purely political meaning to the word "imperialism" in the sense that he, Kautsky, understands it. We take up the work by the English writer Hobson, *Imperialism*, which appeared in 1902, and there we read:

> The new imperialism differs from the older, first, in substituting for the ambition
> of a single growing empire the theory and the practice of competing empires, each
> motivated by similar lusts of political aggrandisement and commercial gain; secondly,
> in the dominance of financial or investing over mercantile interests.[89]

We see that Kautsky is absolutely wrong in referring to English writers generally (unless he meant the vulgar English imperialists, or the avowed apologists for imperialism). We see that Kautsky, while claiming that he continues to advocate Marxism, as a matter of fact takes a step backward compared with the *social-liberal* Hobson, who *more correctly* takes into account two "historically concrete" (Kautsky's definition is a mockery of historical concreteness !) features of modern imperialism: (1) the competition between *several* imperialisms, and (2) the predominance of the financier over the merchant. If it is chiefly a question of the annexation of agrarian countries by industrial countries, then the role of the merchant is put in the forefront.

Kautsky's definition is not only wrong and un-Marxist. It serves as a basis for a whole system of views which signify a rupture with Marxist theory and Marxist practice all along the line. I shall refer to this later. The argument about words which Kautsky raises as to whether the latest stage of capitalism should be called imperialism or the stage of finance capital is not worth serious attention. Call it what you will, it makes no difference. The essence of the matter is that Kautsky detaches the politics of imperialism from its economics, speaks of annexations as being a policy "preferred" by finance capital, and opposes to it another bourgeois policy which, he alleges, is possible on this very same basis of finance capital. It follows, then, that monopolies in the economy are compatible with non-monopolistic, non-violent, non-annexationist methods in politics. It follows, then, that the territorial division of the world, which was completed during this very epoch of finance capital, and which constitutes the basis of the present peculiar forms of rivalry between the biggest capitalist states, is compatible with a non-imperialist policy. The result is a slurring-over and a blunting of the most profound contradictions of the latest stage of capitalism, instead of an exposure of their depth; the result is bourgeois reformism instead of Marxism.

Kautsky enters into controversy with the German apologist of imperialism and annexations, Cunow, who clumsily and cynically argues that imperialism is present-day capitalism; the development of capitalism is inevitable and progressive; therefore imperialism is progressive; therefore, we should grovel before it and glorify it! This is something like the caricature of the Russian Marxists which the Narodniks drew in 1894-95. They argued: if the Marxists believe that capitalism is inevitable in Russia, that it is progressive, then they ought to open a tavern and begin to implant capitalism! Kautsky's reply to Cunow is as follows: imperialism is not present-day capitalism; it is only one of the forms of the policy of present-day capitalism. This policy we can and should fight, fight imperialism, annexations, etc.

The reply seems quite plausible, but in effect it is a more subtle and more disguised (and therefore more dangerous) advocacy of conciliation with imperialism, because a "fight" against the policy of the trusts and banks that does not affect the economic basis of the trusts and banks is mere bourgeois reformism and pacifism, the benevolent and innocent expression of pious wishes. Evasion of existing contradictions, forgetting the most important of them, instead of revealing their full depth — such is Kautsky's theory, which has nothing in common with Marxism. Naturally, such a "theory" can only serve the purpose of advocating unity with the Cunows!

"From the purely economic point of view", writes Kautsky, "it is not impossible that capitalism will yet go through a new phase, that of the extension of the policy of the cartels to foreign policy, the phase of ultra-imperialism",[90] i.e., of a superimperialism, of a union of the imperialisms of the whole world and not struggles among them, a phase when wars shall cease under capitalism, a phase of "the joint exploitation of the world by internationally united finance capital".[91]

We shall have to deal with this "theory of ultra-imperialism" later on in order to show in detail how definitely and utterly it breaks with Marxism. At present, in keeping with the general plan of the present work, we must examine the exact economic data on this question. "From the purely economic point of view", is "ultra-imperialism" possible, or is it ultra-nonsense?

If the purely economic point of view is meant to be a "pure" abstraction is meant, then all that can be said reduces itself to the following proposition: development is proceeding towards monopolies, hence, towards a single world monopoly, towards a single world trust. This is indisputable, but it is also as completely meaningless as is the statement that "development is proceeding" towards the manufacture of foodstuffs in labouratories. In this sense the "theory" of ultra-imperialism is no less absurd than a "theory of ultra-agriculture" would be.

If, however, we are discussing the "purely economic" conditions of the epoch of finance capital as a historically concrete epoch which began at the turn of the 20th century, then the best reply that one can make to the lifeless abstractions of "ultra-imperialism" (which serve exclusively a most reactionary aim: that of diverting attention from the depth of *existing* antagonisms) is to contrast them with the concrete economic realities of present-day world economy. Kautsky's utterly meaningless talk about ultra-imperialism encourages, among other things, that profoundly mistaken idea which only brings grist to the mill of the apologists of imperialism, i.e., that the rule of finance capital *lessens* the unevenness and contradictions inherent in world economy, whereas in reality it *increases* them.

R. Calwer, in his little book, *An Introduction to the World Economy*,[92] made an attempt to summarise the main, purely economic, data that enable one to obtain a concrete picture of the internal relations of world economy at the turn of the 20th century. He divides the world into five "main economic areas", as follows: (1) Central Europe (the whole of Europe with the exception of Russia and Great Britain); (2) Great Britain; (3) Russia; (4) Eastern Asia; (5) America: he includes the colonies in the "areas" of the states to which they belong and "leaves aside" a few countries not distributed according to areas, such as Persia, Afghanistan, and Arabia in Asia, Morocco and Abyssinia in Africa, etc.

Here is a brief summary of the economic data he quotes on these regions:

	Area (mill sq. km.)	Pop. (mill.)	Transport		Trade	Industry		
			Railways (thousand km.)	Merc-antile fleet (mill. tons)	Imports & exports (billion marks)	*Output* (mill. tons)		Number of cotton spindles (mill.)
Principal economic areas						Coal	Iron	
1) Central Europe	27.6 (23.6)	388 (146)	204	8	41	251	15	26
2) Britain	28.9 (28.6)	398 (355)	140	11	25	249	9	51
3) Russia	22	131	63	1	3	16	3	7
4) Eastern Asia	12	389	8	1	2	8	0.02	2
5) America	30	148	379	6	14	245	14	19

(The figures in parentheses show the area and population of the colonies.)

We see three areas of highly developed capitalism (high development of means of transport, of trade and of industry): the Central European, the British and the American areas. Among these are three states which dominate the world: Germany, Great Britain, the United States. Imperialist rivalry and the struggle between these countries have become extremely keen because Germany has only an insignificant area and few colonies; the creation of "Central Europe" is still a matter for the future, it is being born in the midst of a desperate struggle. For the moment the distinctive feature of the whole of Europe is political incohesion. In the British and American areas, on the other hand, political concentration is very highly developed, but there is a vast disparity between the immense colonies of the one and the insignificant colonies of the other. In the colonies, however, capitalism is only beginning to develop. The struggle for South America is becoming more and more acute.

There are two areas where capitalism is little developed: Russia and Eastern Asia. In the former, the population is extremely sparse, in the latter it is extremely dense; in the former political concentration is high, in the latter it does not exist. The partitioning of China is only just beginning, and the struggle for it between Japan, USA, etc. is continually gaining in intensity.

Compare this reality — the vast diversity of economic and political conditions, the extreme disparity in the rate of development of the various countries, etc., and the violent struggles among the imperialist states — with Kautsky's silly little fable about "peaceful" ultra-imperialism. Is this not the reactionary attempt of a frightened philistine to hide from stern reality? Are not the international cartels which Kautsky imagines are the embryos of "ultra-imperialism" (in the same way as one "can" describe the manufacture of tablets in a laboratory as ultra-agriculture in embryo) an example of the division *and the redivision* of the world, the transition from peaceful division to non-peaceful division and vice versa? Is not American and other finance capital, which divided the whole world peacefully with Germany's participation in, for example, the international rail syndicate, or in the international mercantile shipping trust, now engaged in *redividing* the world on the basis of a new relation of forces, that is being changed by methods *anything* but peaceful?

Finance capital and the trusts do not diminish but increase the differences in the rate of growth of the various parts of the world economy. Once the relation of forces is changed, what other solution of the contradictions can be found *under capitalism* than that of *force*? Railway statistics[93] provide remarkably exact data on the different rates of growth of capitalism and finance capital in world economy. In the last decades of imperialist development, the total length of railways has changed as follows:

Railways
(thousand kilometres)

	1890	1913	+
Europe	224	346	+122
USA	268	411	+143
All colonies	82	210	+128
Independent and semi -independent states of	125	347	+222
Asia and America	43	137	+94
Total	617	1,104	

Thus, the development of railways has been most rapid in the colonies and in the independent (and semi-independent) states of Asia and America. Here, as we know, the finance capital of the four or five biggest capitalist states holds undisputed sway. Two hundred thousand kilometres of new railways in the colonies and in the other countries of Asia and America represent a capital of more than 40 billion marks, newly invested on particularly advantageous terms, with special guarantees of a good return and with profitable orders for steel works, etc., etc.

Capitalism is growing with the greatest rapidity in the colonies and in overseas countries. Among the latter, *new* imperialist powers are emerging (e.g., Japan). The struggle among the world imperialisms is becoming more acute. The tribute levied by finance capital on the most profitable colonial and overseas enterprises is increasing. In the division of this "booty", an exceptionally large part goes to countries which do not always stand at the top of the list in the rapidity of the development of their productive forces. In the case of the biggest countries, considered with their colonies, the total length of railways was as follows:

	(thousand kilometres)		
	1890	*1913*	
US	268	413	+145
British Empire	107	208	+101
Russia	32	78	+46
Germany	43	68	+25
France	41	63	+22
Total for five powers	491	830	+339

Thus, about 80% of the total existing railways are concentrated in the hands of the five biggest powers. But the concentration of the *ownership* of these railways, the concentration of finance capital, is immeasurably greater, for the French and British millionaires, for example, own an enormous amount of shares and bonds in American, Russian and other railways.

Thanks to her colonies, Great Britain has increased the length of "her" railways by 100,000 kilometres, four times as much as Germany. And yet, it is well known that the development of productive forces in Germany, and especially the development of the coal and iron industries, has been incomparably more rapid during this period than in Britain — not to speak of France and Russia. In 1892, Germany produced 4,900,000 tons of pig iron and Great Britain produced 6,800,000 tons; in 1912, Germany produced 17,600,000 tons and Great Britain, 9 million tons. Germany, therefore, had an overwhelming superiority over England in this respect.[94] The question is: what means other than war could there be *under capitalism* to overcome the disparity between the development of productive forces and the accumulation of capital on the one side, and the division of colonies and spheres of influence for finance capital on the other? +

VIII

PARASITISM AND DECAY OF CAPITALISM

WE NOW HAVE to examine yet another significant aspect of imperialism to which most of the discussions on this subject usually attach insufficient importance. One of the shortcomings of the Marxist Hilferding is that on this point he has taken a step backward compared with the non-Marxist Hobson. I refer to parasitism, which is characteristic of imperialism.

As we have seen, the deepest economic foundation of imperialism is monopoly. This is capitalist monopoly, i.e., monopoly which has grown out of capitalism and exists in the general environment of capitalism, commodity production and competition, in permanent and insoluble contradiction to this general environment. Nevertheless, like all monopoly, it inevitably engenders a tendency to stagnation and decay. Since monopoly prices are established, even temporarily, the motive cause of technical and, consequently, of all other progress, disappears to a certain extent and, further, the *economic* possibility arises of deliberately retarding technical progress. For instance, in America, a certain Owens invented a machine which revolutionised the manufacture of bottles. The German bottle-manufacturing cartel purchased Owens' patent, but pigeonholed it, refrained from utilising it. Certainly, monopoly under capitalism can never completely, and for a very long period of time, eliminate competition in the world market (and this, by the by, is one of the reasons why the theory of ultra-imperialism is so absurd). Certainly, the possibility of reducing cost of production and increasing profits by introducing technical improvements operates in the direction of change. But the *tendency* to stagnation and decay, which is characteristic of monopoly, continues to operate, and in some branches of industry, in some countries, for certain periods of time, it gains the upper hand.

The monopoly ownership of very extensive, rich or well situated colonies, operates in the same direction.

Further, imperialism is an immense accumulation of money capital in a few countries, amounting, as we have seen, to 100,000-150,000 million francs in securities.

Hence the extraordinary growth of a class, or rather, of a stratum of rentiers, i.e., people who live by "clipping coupons", who take no part in any enterprise whatever, whose profession is idleness. The export of capital, one of the most essential economic bases of imperialism, still more completely isolates the rentiers from production and sets the seal of parasitism on the whole country that lives by exploiting the labour of several overseas countries and colonies.

"In 1893", writes Hobson, "the British capital invested abroad represented about 15% of the total wealth of the United Kingdom."[95] Let me remind the reader that by 1915 this capital had increased about two and a half times. "Aggressive imperialism," says Hobson further on, "which costs the taxpayer so dear, which is of so little value to the manufacturer and trader ... is a source of great gain to the investor... The annual income Great Britain derives from commissions in her whole foreign and colonial trade, import and export, is estimated by Sir R. Giffen at £18 million [nearly 170 million rubles] for 1899, taken at 2½%, upon a turnover of £800 million." Great as this sum is, it cannot explain the aggressive imperialism of Great Britain, which is explained by the income of £90 million to £100 million from "invested" capital, the income of the rentiers.

The income of the rentiers is *five times greater* than the income obtained from the foreign trade of the biggest "trading" country in the world! This is the essence of imperialism and imperialist parasitism.

For that reason the term, "rentier state" (Rentnerstaat), or usurer state, is coming into common use in the economic literature that deals with imperialism. The world has become divided into a handful of usurer states and a vast majority of debtor states. "At the top of the list of foreign investments", says Schulze-Gaevernitz, "are those placed in politically dependent or allied countries: Great Britain grants loans to Egypt, Japan, China and South America. Her navy plays here the part of bailiff in case of necessity. Great Britain's political power protects her from the indignation of her debtors."[96] Sartorius von Waltershausen in his book, *The National Economic System of Capital Investments Abroad*, cites Holland as the model "rentier state" and points out that Great Britain and France are now becoming such.[97] Schilder is of the opinion that five industrial states have become "definitely pronounced creditor countries": Great Britain, France, Germany, Belgium and Switzerland. He does not include Holland in this list simply because she is "industrially little developed".[98] The United States is a creditor only of the American countries.

"Great Britain", says Schulze-Gaevernitz, "is gradually becoming transformed from an industrial into a creditor state. Notwithstanding the absolute increase in industrial output and the export of manufactured goods, there is an increase in the relative importance of income from interest and dividends, issues of securities, commissions and speculation in the whole of the national economy. In my opinion it is precisely this that forms the economic basis of imperialist ascendancy. The creditor is more firmly attached to the debtor than the seller is to the buyer."[99] In regard to Germany, A. Lansburgh, the publisher of the Berlin *Die Bank*, in 1911, in an article entitled "Germany — a Rentier State", wrote the following:

> People in Germany are ready to sneer at the yearning to become rentiers that is observed in France. But they forget that as far as the bourgeoisie is concerned the situation in Germany is becoming more and more like that in France.[100]

The rentier state is a state of parasitic, decaying capitalism, and this circumstance cannot fail to influence all the socio-political conditions of the countries concerned in general, and the two fundamental trends in the working-class movement, in particular. To demonstrate this in the clearest possible manner let me quote Hobson, who is a most "reliable" witness, since he cannot be suspected of leaning towards Marxist orthodoxy; on the other hand, he is an Englishman who is very well acquainted with the situation in the country which is richest in colonies, in finance capital, and in imperialist experience.

With the Anglo-Boer War fresh in his mind, Hobson describes the connection between imperialism and the interests of the "financiers", their growing profits from contracts, supplies, etc., and writes:

> While the directors of this definitely parasitic policy are capitalists, the same motives appeal to special classes of the workers. In many towns, most important trades are dependent upon government employment or contracts; the imperialism of the metal and ship-building centers is attributable in no small degree to this fact.

Two sets of circumstances in this writer's opinion have weakened the old empires: (1) "economic parasitism", and (2) the formation of armies recruited from subject peoples. "There is first the habit of economic parasitism, by which the ruling state has used its provinces, colonies, and dependencies in order to enrich its ruling class and to bribe its lower classes into acquiescence." And I shall add that the economic possibility of such bribery, whatever its form may be, requires high monopolist profits. As for the second circumstance, Hobson writes:

> One of the strangest symptoms of the blindness of imperialism is the reckless indifference with which Great Britain, France and other imperial nations are embarking on this perilous dependence. Great Britain has gone farthest. Most of the fighting by which we have won our Indian Empire has been done by natives; in India, as more

recently in Egypt, great standing armies are placed under British commanders; almost all the fighting associated with our African dominions, except in the southern part, has been done for us by natives.

Hobson gives the following economic appraisal of the prospect of the partitioning of China:

> The greater part of Western Europe might then assume the appearance and character already exhibited by tracts of country in the South of England, in the Riviera, and in the tourist-ridden or residential parts of Italy and Switzerland, little clusters of wealthy aristocrats drawing dividends and pensions from the Far East, with a somewhat larger group of professional retainers and tradesmen and a larger body of personal servants and workers in the transport trade and in the final stages of production of the more perishable goods; all the main arterial industries would have disappeared, the staple foods and manufactures flowing in as tribute from Asia and Africa …

> We have foreshadowed the possibility of even a larger alliance of Western states, a European federation of great powers which, so far from forwarding the cause of world civilisation, might introduce the gigantic peril of a Western parasitism, a group of advanced industrial nations, whose upper classes drew vast tribute from Asia and Africa, with which they supported great tame masses of retainers, no longer engaged in the staple industries of agriculture and manufacture, but kept in the performance of personal or minor industrial services under the control of a new financial aristocracy. Let those who would scout such a theory [it would be better to say: prospect] as undeserving of consideration examine the economic and social condition of districts in southern England today which are already reduced to this condition, and reflect upon the vast extension of such a system which might be rendered feasible by the subjection of China to the economic control of similar groups of financiers, investors, and political and business officials, draining the greatest potential reservoir of profit the world has ever known, in order to consume it in Europe. The situation is far too complex, the play of world forces far too incalculable, to render this or any other single interpretation of the future very probable; but the influences which govern the imperialism of Western Europe today are moving in this direction, and, unless counteracted or diverted, make towards some such consummation.[101]

The author is quite right: *if* the forces of imperialism had not been counteracted they would have led precisely to what he has described. The significance of a "United States of Europe" in the present imperialist situation is correctly appraised. He should have added, however, that, also *within* the working-class movement, the opportunists, who are for the moment victorious in most countries, are "working" systematically and undeviatingly in this very direction. Imperialism, which means the partitioning of the world, and the exploitation of other countries besides China, which means high monopoly profits for a handful of very rich countries, makes it economically possible to bribe the upper strata of the proletariat, and thereby fosters, gives shape to, and strengthens opportunism. We must not, however, lose sight of the forces which counteract imperialism in general, and opportunism in particular, and which, naturally, the social-liberal Hobson is unable to perceive.

The German opportunist, Gerhard Hildebrand, who was once expelled from the Party for defending imperialism, and who could today be a leader of the so-called "Social-Democratic" Party of Germany, supplements Hobson well by his advocacy of a "United States of Western Europe" (without Russia) for the purpose of "joint" action ... against the African Negroes, against the "great Islamic movement", for the maintenance of a "powerful army and navy", against a "Sino-Japanese coalition",[102] etc.

The description of "British imperialism" in Schulze-Gaevernitz's book reveals the same parasitical traits. The national income of Great Britain approximately doubled from 1865 to 1898, while the income "from abroad" increased *ninefold* in the same period. While the "merit" of imperialism is that it "trains the Negro to habits of industry" (you cannot manage without coercion ...), the "danger" of imperialism lies in that "Europe will shift the burden of physical toil — first agricultural and mining, then the rougher work in industry — on to the coloured races, and itself be content with the role of rentier, and in this way, perhaps, pave the way for the economic, and later, the political emancipation of the coloured races."

An increasing proportion of land in Great Britain is being taken out of cultivation and used for sport, for the diversion of the rich. As far as Scotland — the most aristocratic place for hunting and other sports — is concerned it is said that "it lives on its past and on Mr. Carnegie" (the American multimillionaire). On horse racing and fox hunting alone England annually spends £14 million. The number of rentiers in England is about one million. The percentage of the productively employed population to the total population is declining:

	Population England and Wales (millions)	*Workers in basic industries (millions)*	*% of total population*
1851	17.9	4.1	23
1901	32.5	4.9	15

And in speaking of the British working class the bourgeois student of "British imperialism at the beginning of the 20th century" is obliged to distinguish systematically between the "*upper stratum*" of the workers and the "*lower stratum of the proletariat proper*". The upper stratum furnishes the bulk of the membership of cooperatives, of trade unions, of sporting clubs and of numerous religious sects. To this level is adapted the electoral system, which in Great Britain is still "*sufficiently restricted to exclude the lower stratum of the proletariat proper*"! In order to present the condition of the British working class in a rosy light, only this upper stratum — which constitutes a minority of the proletariat — is usually spoken of. For instance, "the problem of unemployment is mainly a London problem and that of the lower proletarian stratum, *to which the politicians attach little importance…*"[103] He should have said: to which the bourgeois politicians and the "socialist" opportunists attach little importance.

One of the special features of imperialism connected with the facts I am describing, is the decline in emigration from imperialist countries and the increase in immigration into these countries from the more backward countries where lower wages are paid. As Hobson observes, emigration from Great Britain has been declining since 1884. In that year the number of emigrants was 242,000, while in 1900, the number was 169,000. Emigration from Germany reached the highest point between 1881 and 1890, with a total of 1,453,000 emigrants. In the course of the following two decades, it fell to 544,000 and to 341,000. On the other hand, there was an increase in the number of workers entering Germany from Austria, Italy, Russia and other countries. According to the 1907 census, there were 1,342,294 foreigners in Germany, of whom 440,800 were industrial workers and 257,329 agricultural workers.[104] In France, the workers employed in the mining industry are, "in great part", foreigners: Poles, Italians and Spaniards.[105] In the United States, immigrants from Eastern and Southern Europe are engaged in the most poorly paid jobs, while American workers provide the highest percentage of overseers or of the better-paid workers.[106] Imperialism has the tendency to create privileged sections also among the workers, and to detach them from the broad masses of the proletariat.

It must be observed that in Great Britain the tendency of imperialism to split the workers, to strengthen opportunism among them and to cause temporary decay in the working-class movement, revealed itself much earlier than the end of the 19th and the beginning of the 20th centuries; for two important distinguishing features of imperialism were already observed in Great Britain in the middle of the 19th century — vast colonial possessions and a monopolist position in the world market. Marx and

Engels traced this connection between opportunism in the working-class movement and the imperialist features of British capitalism systematically, during the course of several decades. For example, on October 7, 1858, Engels wrote to Marx:

> The English proletariat is actually becoming more and more bourgeois, so that this most bourgeois of all nations is apparently aiming ultimately at the possession of a bourgeois aristocracy, and a bourgeois proletariat *alongside* the bourgeoisie. For a nation which exploits the whole world this is, of course, to a certain extent justifiable.

Almost a quarter of a century later, in a letter dated August 11, 1881, Engels speaks of "... the worst English trade unions which allow themselves to be led by men sold to, or at least paid by, the middle class". In a letter to Kautsky, dated September 12, 1882, Engels wrote:

> You ask me what the English workers think about colonial policy? Well, exactly the same as they think about politics in general. There is no workers' party here, there are only Conservatives and Liberal-Radicals, and the workers gaily share the feast of England's monopoly of the world market and the colonies[107] (Engels expressed similar ideas in the press in his preface to the second edition of *The Condition of the Working Class in England*, which appeared in 1892).

This clearly shows the causes and effects. The causes are: (1) exploitation of the whole world by this country; (2) its monopolistic position in the world market; (3) its colonial monopoly. The effects are: (1) a section of the British proletariat becomes bourgeois; (2) a section of the proletariat permits itself to be led by men bought by, or at least paid by, the bourgeoisie. The imperialism of the beginning of the 20th century completed the division of the world among a handful of states, each of which today exploits (in the sense of drawing superprofits from) a part of the "whole world" only a little smaller than that which England exploited in 1858; each of them occupies a monopoly position in the world market thanks to trusts, cartels, finance capital and creditor and debtor relations; each of them enjoys to some degree a colonial monopoly (we have seen that out of the total of 75 million sq. km., which comprise the *whole* colonial world, *65 million* sq. km., or 86%, belong to six powers; *61 million* sq. km., or 81%, belong to three powers).

The distinctive feature of the present situation is the prevalence of such economic and political conditions that are bound to increase the irreconcilability between opportunism and the general and vital interests of the working-class movement: imperialism has grown from the embryo into the predominant system; capitalist monopolies occupy first place in economics and politics; the division of the world has been completed; on the other hand, instead of the undivided monopoly of Great

Britain, we see a few imperialist powers contending for the right to share in this monopoly, and this struggle is characteristic of the whole period of the early 20th century. Opportunism cannot now be completely triumphant in the working-class movement of one country for decades as it was in Britain in the second half of the 19th century; but in a number of countries it has grown ripe, overripe, and rotten, and has become completely merged with bourgeois policy in the form of "social chauvinism".[108]+

IX

CRITIQUE OF IMPERIALISM

BY THE CRITIQUE OF IMPERIALISM, in the broad sense of the term, we mean the attitude of the different classes of society towards imperialist policy in connection with their general ideology.

The enormous dimensions of finance capital concentrated in a few hands and creating an extraordinarily dense and widespread network of relationships and connections which subordinates not only the small and medium, but also the very small capitalists and small masters, on the one hand, and the increasingly intense struggle waged against other national state groups of financiers for the division of the world and domination over other countries, on the other hand, cause the propertied classes to go over entirely to the side of imperialism. "General" enthusiasm over the prospects of imperialism, furious defense of it and painting it in the brightest colours — such are the signs of the times. Imperialist ideology also penetrates the working class. No Chinese Wall separates it from the other classes. The leaders of the present-day, so-called, "Social-Democratic" Party of Germany are justly called "social-imperialists", that is, socialists in words and imperialists in deeds; but as early as 1902, Hobson noted the existence in England of "Fabian imperialists" who belonged to the opportunist Fabian Society.

Bourgeois scholars and publicists usually come out in defense of imperialism in a somewhat veiled form; they obscure its complete domination and its deep-going roots, strive to push specific and secondary details into the forefront and do their very best to distract attention from essentials by means of absolutely ridiculous schemes for "reform", such as police supervision of the trusts or banks, etc. Cynical and frank imperialists who are bold enough to admit the absurdity of the idea of reforming the fundamental characteristics of imperialism are a rarer phenomenon..

Here is an example. The German imperialists attempt, in the magazine *Archives of World Economy* to follow the national emancipation movements in the colonies, particularly, of course, in colonies other than those belonging to Germany. They note the unrest and the protest movements in India, the movement in Natal (South Africa), in the Dutch East Indies, etc. One of them, commenting on an English report of a conference held on June 28-30, 1910, of representatives of various subject nations and races, of peoples of Asia, Africa and Europe who are under foreign rule, writes as follows in appraising the speeches delivered at this conference:

> We are told that we must fight imperialism, that the ruling states should recognise the right of subject peoples to independence, that an international tribunal should supervise the fulfilment of treaties concluded between the great powers and weak peoples. Further than the expression of these pious wishes they do not go. We see no trace of understanding of the fact that imperialism is inseparably bound up with capitalism in its present form and that, therefore [!!], an open struggle against imperialism would be hopeless, unless, perhaps, the fight were to be confined to protests against certain of its especially abhorrent excesses.[109]

Since the reform of the basis of imperialism is a deception, a "pious wish", since the bourgeois representatives of the oppressed nations go no "further" forward, the bourgeois representative of an oppressing nation goes "further" *backward*, to servility towards imperialism under cover of the claim to be "scientific". That is also "logic"!

The questions as to whether it is possible to reform the basis of imperialism, whether to go forward to the further intensification and deepening of the antagonisms which it engenders, or backwards, towards allaying these antagonisms, are fundamental questions in the critique of imperialism. Since the specific political features of imperialism are reaction everywhere and increased national oppression due to the oppression of the financial oligarchy and the elimination of free competition, a petty-bourgeois-democratic opposition to imperialism arose in the beginning of the 20th century in nearly all imperialist countries. Kautsky not only did not trouble to oppose, was not only unable to oppose this petty-bourgeois reformist opposition, which is really reactionary in its economic basis, but became merged with it in practice, and this is precisely where Kautsky and the broad international Kautskian trend deserted Marxism.

In the United States, the imperialist war waged against Spain in 1898 stirred up the opposition of the "anti-imperialists", the last of the Mohicans of bourgeois democracy, who declared this war to be "criminal", regarded the annexation of foreign territories as a violation of the Constitution, declared that the treatment of Aguinaldo, leader of the Filipinos (the Americans promised him the independence of his country, but later landed troops and annexed it) was "Jingo treachery", and quoted the words of

Lincoln: "When the white man governs himself, that is self-government; but when he governs himself and also governs others, it is no longer self-government; it is despotism."[110] But as long as all this criticism shrank from recognising the inseverable bond between imperialism and the trusts, and, therefore, between imperialism and the foundations of capitalism, while it shrank from joining the forces engendered by large-scale capitalism and its development — it remained a "pious wish".

This is also the main attitude taken by Hobson in his critique of imperialism. Hobson anticipated Kautsky in protesting against the "inevitability of imperialism" argument, and in urging the necessity of "increasing the consuming capacity" of the people (under capitalism!). The petty-bourgeois point of view in the critique of imperialism, the omnipotence of the banks, the financial oligarchy, etc., is adopted by the authors we have often quoted, such as Agahd, A. Lansburgh, L. Eschwege, and among the French writers, Victor Berard, author of a superficial book entitled *England and Imperialism* which appeared in 1900. All these authors, who make no claim to be Marxists, contrast imperialism with free competition and democracy, condemn the Baghdad railway scheme as leading to conflicts and war, utter "pious wishes" for peace, etc. This applies also to the compiler of international stock and share issue statistics, A. Neymarck, who, after calculating the thousands of millions of francs representing "international" securities, exclaimed in 1912: "Is it possible to believe that peace may be disturbed ... that, in the face of these enormous figures, anyone would risk starting a war?"[111]

Such simple-mindedness on the part of the bourgeois economists is not surprising; moreover, *it is in their interest* to pretend to be so naive and to talk "seriously" about peace under imperialism. But what remains of Kautsky's Marxism, when, in 1914, 1915 and 1916, he takes up the same bourgeois-reformist point of view and affirms that "everybody is agreed" (imperialists, pseudo-socialists and social-pacifists) on the matter of peace? Instead of an analysis of imperialism and an exposure of the depths of its contradictions, we have nothing but a reformist "pious wish" to wave them aside, to evade them.

Here is a sample of Kautsky's economic criticism of imperialism. He takes the statistics of the British export and import trade with Egypt for 1872 and 1912; it seems that this export and import trade has grown more slowly than British foreign trade as a whole. From this Kautsky concludes that "we have no reason to suppose that without military occupation the growth of British trade with Egypt would have been less, simply as a result of the mere operation of economic factors ... The urge of capital to expand ... can be best promoted, not by the violent methods of imperialism, but by peaceful democracy".[112]

This argument of Kautsky's which is repeated in every key by his Russian armour-bearer (and Russian shielder of the social-chauvinists), Mr. Spectator, constitutes the basis of Kautskian critique of imperialism, and that is why we must deal with it in greater detail. We will begin with a quotation from Hilferding, whose conclusions Kautsky on many occasions, and notably in April 1915, has declared to have been "unanimously adopted by all socialist theoreticians".

"It is not the business of the proletariat", writes Hilferding, "to contrast the more progressive capitalist policy with that of the now bygone era of free trade and of hostility towards the state. The reply of the proletariat to the economic policy of finance capital, to imperialism, cannot be free trade, but socialism. The aim of proletarian policy cannot now be the ideal of restoring free competition — which has now become a reactionary ideal — but the complete elimination of competition by the abolition of capitalism."[113]

Kautsky broke with Marxism by advocating in the epoch of finance capital a "reactionary ideal", "peaceful democracy", "the mere operation of economic factors", for *objectively* this ideal drags us back from monopoly to non-monopolist capitalism, and is a reformist swindle.

Trade with Egypt (or with any other colony or semicolony) "would have grown more" *without* military occupation, without imperialism, and without finance capital. What does this mean? That capitalism would have developed more rapidly if free competition had not been restricted by monopolies in general, or by the "connections", yoke (i.e., also the monopoly) of finance capital, or by the monopolist possession of colonies by certain countries?

Kautsky's argument can have no other meaning, and *this* "meaning" is meaningless. Let us assume that free competition, without any sort of monopoly, *would* have developed capitalism and trade more rapidly. But the more rapidly trade and capitalism develop, the greater is the concentration of production and capital which *gives rise* to monopoly. And monopolies have *already* arisen — precisely *out* of free competition! Even if monopolies have now begun to retard progress, it is not an argument in favour of free competition, which has become impossible after it has given rise to monopoly.

Whichever way one turns Kautsky's argument, one will find nothing in it except reaction and bourgeois reformism.

Even if we correct this argument and say, as Spectator says, that the trade of the colonies with Britain is now developing more slowly than their trade with other countries, it does not save Kautsky; for it is *also* monopoly, *also* imperialism that is beating Great Britain, only it is the monopoly and imperialism of another country (America, Germany). It is known that the cartels have given rise to a new and peculiar form of protective tariffs, i.e., goods suitable for export are protected (Engels noted this in Vol. III of *Capital*). It is known, too, that the cartels and finance capital have a system peculiar to themselves, that of "exporting goods at cut-rate prices", or "dumping", as the English call it: within a given country the cartel sells its goods at high monopoly prices, but sells them abroad at a much lower price to undercut the competitor, to enlarge its own production to the utmost, etc. If Germany's trade with the British colonies is developing more rapidly than Great Britain's, it only proves that German imperialism is younger, stronger and better organised than British imperialism, is superior to it; but it by no means proves the "superiority" of free trade, for it is not a fight between free trade and protection and colonial dependence, but between two rival imperialisms, two monopolies, two groups of finance capital. The superiority of German imperialism over British imperialism is more potent than the wall of colonial frontiers or of protective tariffs: to use this as an "argument" *in favour* of free trade and "peaceful democracy" is banal, it means forgetting the essential features and characteristics of imperialism, substituting petty-bourgeois reformism for Marxism.

It is interesting to note that even the bourgeois economist, A. Lansburgh, whose criticism of imperialism is as petty-bourgeois as Kautsky's, nevertheless got closer to a more scientific study of trade statistics. He did not compare one single country, chosen at random, and one single colony with the other countries; he examined the export trade of an imperialist country: (1) with countries which are financially dependent upon it, and borrow money from it; and (2) with countries which are financially independent. He obtained the following results:

Export trade of Germany
(million marks)

		1889	1908	% increase
To countries	Romania	48.2	70.8	47
financially	Portugal	19.0	32.8	73
dependent	Argentina	60.7	147.0	143
on	Brazil	48.7	84.5	73
Germany	Chile	28.3	52.4	85
	Turkey	29.9	64.0	114
	Total	*234.8*	*451.5*	*92*
To countries	Great Britain	651.8	997.4	53
financially	France	210.2	437.9	108
independent	Belgium	137.2	322.8	135
of	Switzerland	177.4	401.1	127
Germany	Australia	21.2	64.5	205
	Dutch East Indies	8.8	40.7	363
	Total	*1206.6*	*2264.4*	*87*

Lansburgh did not draw *conclusions* and therefore, strangely enough, failed to observe that *if* the figures prove anything at all, they prove that *he is wrong* for the exports to countries financially dependent on Germany have grown *more rapidly*, if only slightly, than exports to the countries which are financially independent. (I emphasise the "if", for Lansburgh's figures are far from complete.)

Tracing the connection between exports and loans, Lansburgh writes:

In 1890-91 a Romanian loan was floated through the German banks, which had already in previous years made advances on this loan. It was used chiefly to purchase railway materials in Germany. In 1891 German exports to Romania amounted to 55 million marks. The following year they dropped to 39,400,000 marks and, with fluctuations, to 25,400,000 in 1900. Only in very recent years have they regained the level of 1891 thanks to two new loans.

German exports to Portugal rose, following the loans of 1888-89, to 21,100,000 (1890); then, in the two following years, they dropped to 16,200,000 and 7,400,000, and regained their former level only in 1903.

The figures of German trade with Argentina are still more striking. Loans were floated in 1888 and 1890, German exports to Argentina reached 60,700,000 marks (1889). Two years later they amounted to only 18,600,000 marks, less than one-third of the previous figure. It was not until 1901 that they regained and surpassed the level of 1889, and then only as a result of new loans floated by the state and by municipalities, with advances to build power stations, and with other credit operations.

Exports to Chile, as a consequence of the loan of 1889, rose to 45,200,000 marks (in 1892) and a year later dropped to 22,500,000 marks. A new Chilean loan floated by the German banks in 1906 was followed by a rise of exports to 84,700,000 marks in 1907, only to fall again to 52,400,000 marks in 1908.[114]

From these facts Lansburgh draws the amusing petty-bourgeois moral of how unstable and irregular export trade is when it is bound up with loans, how bad it is to invest capital abroad instead of "naturally" and "harmoniously" developing home industry, how "costly" are the millions in bakhshish that Krupp has to pay in floating foreign loans; etc. But the facts tell us clearly: the increase in exports is connected with *just these* swindling tricks of finance capital, which is not concerned with bourgeois morality, but with skinning the ox twice — first, it pockets the profits from the loan; then it pockets other profits from the *same* loan which the borrower uses to make purchases from Krupp, or to purchase railway material from the Steel Syndicate, etc.

I repeat that I do not by any means consider Lansburgh's figures to be perfect; but I had to quote them because they are more scientific than Kautsky's and Spectator's, and because Lansburgh showed the correct way to approach the question. In discussing the significance of finance capital in regard to exports, etc., one must be able to single out the connection of exports especially and solely with the tricks of the financiers, especially and solely with the sale of goods by cartels, etc. Simply to compare colonies with non-colonies, one imperialism with another imperialism, one semicolony or colony (Egypt) with all other countries, is to evade and to obscure the very *essence* of the question.

Kautsky's theoretical critique of imperialism has nothing in common with Marxism and serves only as a preamble to propaganda for peace and unity with the opportunists and the social-chauvinists, precisely for the reason that it evades and obscures the very profound and fundamental contradictions of imperialism: the contradictions between monopoly and free competition which exists side by side with it, between the gigantic "operations" (and gigantic profits) of finance capital and "honest" trade in the free market, the contradiction between cartels and trusts, on the one hand, and non-cartelised industry, on the other, etc.

The notorious theory of "ultra-imperialism", invented by Kautsky, is just as reactionary. Compare his arguments on this subject in 1915, with Hobson's arguments in 1902.

Kautsky: "...Cannot the present imperialist policy be supplanted by a new, ultra-imperialist policy, which will introduce the joint exploitation of the world by internationally united finance capital in place of the mutual rivalries of national finance capitals? Such a new phase of capitalism is at any rate conceivable. Can it be achieved? Sufficient premises are still lacking to enable us to answer this question."[115]

Hobson: "Christendom thus laid out in a few great federal empires, each with a retinue of uncivilised dependencies, seems to many the most legitimate development of present tendencies, and one which would offer the best hope of permanent peace on an assured basis of inter-Imperialism."

Kautsky called ultra-imperialism or super-imperialism what Hobson, 13 years earlier, described as inter-imperialism. Except for coining a new and clever catchword, replacing one Latin prefix by another, the only progress Kautsky has made in the sphere of "scientific" thought is that he gave out as Marxism what Hobson, in effect, described as the cant of English parsons. After the Anglo-Boer War it was quite natural for this highly honourable caste to exert their main efforts to *console* the British middle class and the workers who had lost many of their relatives on the battlefields of South Africa and who were obliged to pay higher taxes in order to guarantee still higher profits for the British financiers. And what better consolation could there be than the theory that imperialism is not so bad; that it stands close to inter- (or ultra-) imperialism, which can ensure permanent peace? No matter what the good intentions of the English parsons, or of sentimental Kautsky, may have been, the only objective, i.e., real, social significance of Kautsky's "theory" is this: it is a most reactionary method of consoling the masses with hopes of permanent peace being possible under capitalism, by distracting their attention from the sharp antagonisms and acute problems of the present times, and directing it towards illusory prospects of an imaginary "ultra-imperialism" of the future. Deception of the masses — that is all there is in Kautsky's "Marxist" theory.

Indeed, it is enough to compare well-known and indisputable facts to become convinced of the utter falsity of the prospects which Kautsky tries to conjure up before the German workers (and the workers of all lands). Let us consider India, Indo-China and China. It is known that these three colonial and semicolonial countries, with a population of 600-700 million, are subjected to the exploitation of the finance capital of several imperialist powers: Great Britain, France, Japan, the USA, etc. Let us assume that these imperialist countries form alliances against one another in order to protect or enlarge their possessions, their interests and their spheres of influence in these Asiatic states; these alliances will be "inter-imperialist", or "ultra-imperialist" alliances. Let us assume that *all* the imperialist countries conclude an alliance for the "peaceful" division of these parts of Asia; this alliance would be an alliance of "internationally united finance capital". There are actual examples of alliances of this kind in the history of the 20th century — the attitude of the powers to China, for instance. We ask, is it "conceivable", assuming that the capitalist system remains intact — and this is precisely the assumption that Kautsky does make — that such alliances would be more than temporary, that they would eliminate friction, conflicts and struggle in every possible form?

The question has only to be presented clearly for any other than a negative answer to be impossible. This is because the only conceivable basis under capitalism for the division of spheres of influence, interests, colonies, etc., is a calculation of the *strength* of those participating in the division, their general economic, financial, military strength, etc. And the strength of these participants in the division does not change to an equal degree, for the *even* development of different undertakings, trusts, branches of industry, or countries is impossible under capitalism. Half a century ago Germany was a miserable, insignificant country, if her capitalist strength is compared with that of Britain at that time; Japan compared with Russia in the same way. Is it "conceivable" that in 10 or 20 years' time the relative strength of the imperialist powers will have remained *un*changed? It is out of the question.

Therefore, in the realities of the capitalist system, and not in the banal philistine fantasies of English parsons, or of the German "Marxist", Kautsky, "inter-imperialist" or "ultra-imperialist" alliances, no matter what form they may assume, whether of one imperialist coalition against another, or of a general alliance embracing *all* the imperialist powers, are *inevitably* nothing more than a "truce" in periods between wars. Peaceful alliances prepare the ground for wars, and in their turn grow out of wars; the one conditions the other, producing alternating forms of peaceful and non-peaceful struggle on *one and the same* basis of imperialist connections and relations within world economics and world politics. But in order to pacify the workers and to reconcile them with the social-chauvinists who have deserted to the side of the bourgeoisie, over-wise Kautsky *separates* one link of a single chain from another, separates the present peaceful (and ultra-imperialist, nay, ultra-ultra-imperialist) alliance of *all* the powers for the "pacification" of China (remember the suppression of the Boxer Rebellion) from the non-peaceful conflict of tomorrow, which will prepare the ground for another "peaceful" general alliance for the partition, say, of Turkey, on the day after tomorrow, *etc.*, *etc.* Instead of showing the living connection between periods of imperialist peace and periods of imperialist war, Kautsky presents the workers with a lifeless abstraction in order to reconcile them to their lifeless leaders.

An American writer, Hill, in his *A History of the Diplomacy in the International*

Development of Europe refers in his preface to the following periods in the recent history of diplomacy: (1) the era of revolution; (2) the constitutional movement; (3) the present era of "commercial imperialism".[116] Another writer divides the history of Great Britain's "world policy" since 1870 into four periods: (1) the first Asiatic period (that of the struggle against Russia's advance in Central Asia towards India); (2) the African period (approximately 1885-1902): that of the struggle against France for the partition of Africa (the "Fashoda incident" of 1898 which brought her within a hair's breadth of war with France); (3) the second Asiatic period (alliance with Japan against Russia), and (4) the "European" period, chiefly anti-German.[117] "The political patrol clashes take place on the financial field", wrote the banker Riesser, in 1905, in showing how French finance capital operating in Italy was preparing the way for a political alliance of these countries, and how a conflict was developing between Germany and Great Britain over Persia, between all the European capitalists over Chinese loans, etc. Behold, the living reality of peaceful "ultra-imperialist" alliances in their inseverable connection with ordinary imperialist conflicts!

Kautsky's obscuring of the deepest contradictions of imperialism, which inevitably boils down to painting imperialism in bright colours, leaves its traces in this writer's criticism of the political features of imperialism. Imperialism is the epoch of finance capital and of monopolies, which introduce everywhere the striving for domination, not for freedom. Whatever the political system, the result of these tendencies is everywhere reaction and an extreme intensification of antagonisms in this field. Particularly intensified become the yoke of national oppression and the striving for annexations, i.e., the violation of national independence (for annexation is nothing but the violation of the right of nations to self-determination). Hilferding rightly notes the connection between imperialism and the intensification of national oppression:

> In the newly opened-up countries the capital imported into them intensifies antagonisms and excites against the intruders the constantly growing resistance of the peoples who are awakening to national consciousness; this resistance can easily develop into dangerous measures against foreign capital. The old social relations become completely revolutionised, the age-long agrarian isolation of "nations without history" is destroyed and they are drawn into the capitalist whirlpool. Capitalism itself gradually provides the subjugated with the means and resources for their emancipation and they set out to achieve the goal which once seemed highest to the European nations: the creation of a united national state as a means to economic and cultural freedom. This movement for national independence threatens European capital in its most valuable and most promising fields of exploitation, and European capital can maintain its domination

only by continually increasing its military forces.[118]

To this must be added that it is not only in newly opened up countries, but also in the old, that imperialism is leading to annexation, to increased national oppression, and, consequently, also to increasing resistance. While objecting to the intensification of political reaction by imperialism, Kautsky leaves in the shade a question that has become particularly urgent, viz., the impossibility of unity with the opportunists in the epoch of imperialism. While objecting to annexations, he presents his objections in a form that is most acceptable and least offensive to the opportunists. He addresses himself to a German audience, yet he obscures the most topical and important point, for instance, the annexation of Alsace-Lorraine by Germany. In order to appraise this "mental aberration" of Kautsky's I shall take the following example. Let us suppose that a Japanese condemns the annexation of the Philippines by the Americans. The question is: will many believe that he does so because he has a horror of annexations as such, and not because he himself has a desire to annex the Philippines? And shall we not be constrained to admit that the "fight" the Japanese is waging against annexations can be regarded as being sincere and politically honest only if he fights against the annexation of Korea by Japan, and urges freedom for Korea to secede from Japan?

Kautsky's theoretical analysis of imperialism, as well as his economic and political criticism of imperialism, are permeated *through and through*, with a spirit, absolutely irreconcilable with Marxism, of obscuring and glossing over the fundamental contradictions of imperialism and with a striving to preserve at all costs the crumbling unity with opportunism in the European working-class movement. +

X
THE PLACE OF IMPERIALISM IN HISTORY

WE HAVE SEEN that in its economic essence imperialism is monopoly capitalism. This in itself determines its place in history, for monopoly that grows out of the soil of free competition, and precisely out of free competition, is the transition from the capitalist system to a higher socio-economic order. We must take special note of the four principal types of monopoly, or principal manifestations of monopoly capitalism, which are characteristic of the epoch we are examining.

Firstly, monopoly arose out of the concentration of production at a very high stage. This refers to the monopolist capitalist associations, cartels, syndicates and trusts. We have seen the important part these play in present-day economic life. At the beginning of the 20th century, monopolies had acquired complete supremacy in the advanced countries, and although the first steps towards the formation of the cartels were taken by countries enjoying the protection of high tariffs (Germany, America), Great Britain, with her system of free trade, revealed the same basic phenomenon, only a little later, namely, the birth of monopoly out of the concentration of production.

Secondly, monopolies have stimulated the seizure of the most important sources of raw materials, especially for the basic and most highly cartelised industries in capitalist society: the coal and iron industries. The monopoly of the most important sources of raw materials has enormously increased the power of big capital, and has sharpened the antagonism between cartelised and non-cartelised industry.

Thirdly, monopoly has sprung from the banks. The banks have developed from humble middleman enterprises into the monopolists of finance capital. Some three to five of the biggest banks in each of the foremost capitalist countries have achieved the "personal link-up" between industrial and bank capital, and have concentrated in their hands the control of thousands upon thousands of millions which form the greater part of the capital and income of entire countries. A financial oligarchy, which throws a close network of dependence relationships over all the economic and political institutions of present-day bourgeois society without exception — such is the most striking manifestation of this monopoly.

Fourthly, monopoly has grown out of colonial policy. To the numerous "old" motives of colonial policy, finance capital has added the struggle for the sources of raw materials, for the export of capital, for "spheres of influence", i.e., for spheres for profitable deals, concessions, monopoly profits and so on, economic territory in general. When the colonies of the European powers, for instance, comprised only one-tenth of the territory of Africa (as was the case in 1876), colonial policy was able to develop by methods other than those of monopoly — by the "free grabbing" of territories, so to speak. But when nine-tenths of Africa had been seized (by 1900), when the whole world had been divided up, there was inevitably ushered in the era of monopoly possession of colonies and, consequently, of particularly intense struggle for the division and the redivision of the world.

The extent to which monopolist capital has intensified all the contradictions of capitalism is generally known. It is sufficient to mention the high cost of living and the tyranny of the cartels. This intensification of contradictions constitutes the most powerful driving force of the transitional period of history, which began from the time of the final victory of world finance capital.

Monopolies, oligarchy, the striving for domination and not for liberty, the exploitation of an increasing number of small or weak nations by a handful of the richest or most powerful nations — all these have given birth to those distinctive characteristics of imperialism which compel us to define it as parasitic or decaying capitalism. More and more prominently there emerges, as one of the tendencies of imperialism, the creation of the "rentier state", the usurer state, in which the bourgeoisie to an ever-increasing degree lives on the proceeds of capital exports and by "clipping coupons". It would be a mistake to believe that this tendency to decay precludes the rapid growth of capitalism. It does not. In the epoch of imperialism, certain branches of industry, certain strata of the bourgeoisie and certain countries betray, to a greater or lesser degree, now one and now another of these tendencies. On the whole, capitalism is growing far more rapidly than before; but this growth is not only becoming more and more uneven in general, its unevenness also manifests itself, in particular, in the decay of the countries which are richest in capital (Britain).

In regard to the rapidity of Germany's economic development, Riesser, the author of the book on the big German banks, states:

> The progress of the preceding period (1848-70), which had not been exactly slow, compares with the rapidity with which the whole of Germany's national economy, and with it German banking, progressed during this period (1870-1905) in about the same

way as the speed of the mail coach in the good old days compares with the speed of the present-day automobile ... which is whizzing past so fast that it endangers not only innocent pedestrians in its path, but also the occupants of the car.

In its turn, this finance capital which has grown with such extraordinary rapidity is not unwilling, precisely because it has grown so quickly, to pass on to a more "tranquil" possession of colonies which have to be seized — and not only by peaceful methods — from richer nations. In the United States, economic development in the last decades has been even more rapid than in Germany, *and for this very reason*, the parasitic features of modern American capitalism have stood out with particular prominence. On the other hand, a comparison of, say, the republican American bourgeoisie with the monarchist Japanese or German bourgeoisie shows that the most pronounced political distinction diminishes to an extreme degree in the epoch of imperialism — not because it is unimportant in general, but because in all these cases we are talking about a bourgeoisie which has definite features of parasitism.

The receipt of high monopoly profits by the capitalists in one of the numerous branches of industry, in one of the numerous countries, etc., makes it economically possible for them to bribe certain sections of the workers, and for a time a fairly considerable minority of them, and win them to the side of the bourgeoisie of a given industry or given nation against all the others. The intensification of antagonisms between imperialist nations for the division of the world increases this urge. And so there is created that bond between imperialism and opportunism, which revealed itself first and most clearly in Great Britain, owing to the fact that certain features of imperialist development were observable there much earlier than in other countries. Some writers, L. Martov, for example, are prone to wave aside the connection between imperialism and opportunism in the working-class movement — a particularly glaring fact at the present time — by resorting to "official optimism" (*à la* Kautsky and Huysmans) like the following: the cause of the opponents of capitalism would be hopeless if it were progressive capitalism that led to the increase of opportunism, or, if it were the best paid workers who were inclined towards opportunism, etc. We must have no illusions about "optimism" of this kind. It is optimism in regard to opportunism; it is optimism which serves to conceal opportunism. As a matter of fact the extraordinary rapidity and the particularly revolting character of the development of opportunism is by no means a guarantee that its victory will be durable: the rapid growth of a painful abscess on a healthy body can only cause it to burst more quickly and thus relieve the body of it. The most dangerous of all in this respect are those who do not wish to understand that the fight against imperialism is a sham and humbug unless it is inseparably bound up with the fight against opportunism.

From all that has been said in this book on the economic essence of imperialism, it follows that we must define it as capitalism in transition, or, more precisely, as moribund capitalism. It is very instructive in this respect to note that the bourgeois economists, in describing modern capitalism, frequently employ catchwords and phrases like "interlocking", "absence of isolation", etc.; "in conformity with their functions and course of development", banks are "not purely private business enterprises; they are more and more outgrowing the sphere of purely private business regulation". And this very Riesser, whose words I have just quoted, declares with all seriousness that the "prophecy" of the Marxists concerning "socialisation" has "not come true"!

What then does this catchword "interlocking" express? It merely expresses the most striking feature of the process going on before our eyes. It shows that the observer counts the separate trees, but cannot see the wood. It slavishly copies the superficial, the fortuitous, the chaotic. It reveals the observer as one who is overwhelmed by the mass of raw material and is utterly incapable of appreciating its meaning and importance. Ownership of shares, the relations between owners of private property "interlock in a haphazard way". But underlying this interlocking, its very base, are the changing social relations of production. When a big enterprise assumes gigantic proportions, and, on the basis of an exact computation of mass data, organises according to plan the supply of primary raw materials to the extent of two-thirds, or three-fourths of all that is necessary for tens of millions of people; when the raw materials are transported in a systematic and organised manner to the most suitable place of production, sometimes situated hundreds or thousands of miles from each other, when a single centre directs all the consecutive stages of processing the material right up to the manufacture of numerous varieties of finished articles; when these products are distributed according to a single plan among tens and hundreds of millions of consumers (the marketing of oil in America and Germany by the American "oil trust") — then it becomes evident that we have socialisation of production, and not mere "interlocking"; that private economic and private property relations constitute a shell which no longer fits its contents, a shell which must inevitably decay if its removal is artificially delayed; a shell which may remain in a state of decay for a fairly long period (if, at the worst, the cure of the opportunist abscess is protracted), but which will inevitably be removed.

The enthusiastic admirer of German imperialism, Schulze-Gaevernitz exclaims:

Once the supreme management of the German banks has been entrusted to the hands of a dozen persons, their activity is even today more significant for the public good than that of the majority of the Ministers of State. [The "interlocking" of bankers, ministers, magnates of industry and rentiers is here conveniently forgotten.] ... If we imagine the development of those tendencies we have noted carried to their logical conclusion we will have: the money capital of the nation united in the banks; the banks themselves combined into cartels; the investment capital of the nation cast in the shape of securities. Then the forecast of that genius Saint-Simon will be fulfilled: "The present anarchy of production, which corresponds to the fact that economic relations are developing without uniform regulation, must make way for organisation in production. Production will no longer be directed by isolated manufacturers, independent of each other and ignorant of man's economic needs; that will be done by a certain public institution. A central committee of management, being able to survey the large field of social economy from a more elevated point of view, will regulate it for the benefit of the whole of society, will put the means of production into suitable hands, and above all will take care that there be constant harmony between production and consumption. Institutions already exist which have assumed as part of their functions a certain organisation of economic labour: the banks." We are still a long way from the fulfilment of Saint-Simon's forecast, but we are on the way towards it: Marxism, different from what Marx imagined, but different only in form.[119]

A crushing "refutation" of Marx, indeed, which retreats a step from Marx's precise, scientific analysis to Saint-Simon's guess-work, the guess-work of a genius, but guess-work all the same. +

IMPERIALISM AND THE SPLIT IN SOCIALISM

By V.I. Lenin

IS THERE ANY CONNECTION between imperialism and the monstrous and disgusting victory opportunism (in the form of social-chauvinism) has gained over the labour movement in Europe.

This is the fundamental question of modern socialism. And having in our Party literature fully established, first, the imperialist character of our era and of the present war, and, second, the inseparable historical connection between social-chauvinism and opportunism, as well as the intrinsic similarity of their political ideology, we can and must proceed to analyse this fundamental question.

We have to begin with as precise and full a definition of imperialism as possible. Imperialism is a specific historical stage of capitalism. Its specific character is threefold: imperialism is (1) monopoly capitalism; (2) parasitic, or decaying capitalism; (3) moribund capitalism. The supplanting of free competition by monopoly is the fundamental economic feature, the *quintessence* of imperialism. Monopoly manifests itself in five principal forms: (1) cartels, syndicates and trusts — the concentration of production has reached a degree which gives rise to these monopolistic associations of capitalists; (2) the monopolistic position of the big banks — three, four or five giant banks manipulate the whole economic life of America. France, Germany; (3) seizure of the sources of *raw material* by the trusts and the financial oligarchy (finance capital is monopoly industrial capital merged with bank capital); (4) the (economic) partition of the world by the international cartels has *begun*. There are already over *100* such international cartels, which command the *entire* world market and divide it "amicably" among themselves — until war *re*divides it. The export of capital, as distinct from the export of commodities under non-monopoly capitalism, is a highly characteristic phenomenon and is closely linked with the economic and territorial-political partition of the world; (5) the territorial partition of the world (colonies) is *completed*.

Imperialism, as the highest stage of capitalism in America and Europe, and later in Asia, took final shape in the period 1898-1914. The Spanish-American War (1898), the Anglo-Boer War (1899-1902), the Russo-Japanese War (1904-05) and the economic crisis in Europe in 1900 are the chief historical landmarks in the new era of world history.

The fact that imperialism is parasitic or decaying capitalism is manifested first of all in the tendency to decay, which is characteristic of *every* monopoly under the system of private ownership of the means of production. The difference between the democratic-republican and the reactionary-monarchist imperialist bourgeoisie is obliterated precisely because they are both rotting alive (which by no means precludes an extraordinarily rapid development of capitalism in individual branches of industry, in individual countries, and in individual periods). Secondly, the decay of capitalism is manifested in the creation of a huge stratum of *rentiers*, capitalists who live by "clipping coupons". In each of the four leading imperialist countries — England, USA, France and Germany — capital in securities amounts to 100,000 or 150,000 *million* francs, from which each country derives an annual income of no less than five to eight thousand million. Thirdly, export of capital is parasitism raised to a high pitch. Fourthly, "finance capital strives for domination, not freedom". Political reaction *all along* the line is a characteristic feature of imperialism. Corruption, bribery on a huge scale and all kinds of fraud. Fifthly, the exploitation of oppressed nations — which is inseparably connected with annexations — and especially the exploitation of colonies by a handful of "Great" Powers, increasingly transforms the "civilised" world into a parasite on the body of hundreds of millions in the uncivilised nations. The Roman proletarian lived at the expense of society. Modern society lives at the expense of the modern proletarian. Marx specially stressed this profound observation of Sismondi. Imperialism somewhat changes the situation. A privileged upper stratum of the proletariat in the imperialist countries lives partly at the expense of hundreds of millions in the uncivilised nations.

It is clear why imperialism is *moribund* capitalism, capitalism in *transition* to socialism: monopoly, which grows *out of* capitalism, is *already* dying capitalism, the beginning of its transition to socialism. The tremendous *socialisation* of labour by imperialism (what its apologists — the bourgeois economists — call "interlocking") produces the same result.

Advancing this definition of imperialism brings us into complete contradiction to K. Kautsky, who refuses to regard imperialism as a "phase of capitalism" and defines it as a *policy* "preferred" by finance capital, a tendency of "industrial" countries to annex "agrarian" countries.* Kautsky's definition is thoroughly false from the theoretical standpoint. What distinguishes imperialism is the rule *not* of industrial capital, but of finance capital, the striving to annex *not* agrarian countries, particularly, but *every kind* of country. Kautsky *divorces* imperialist politics from imperialist economics, he divorces monopoly in politics from monopoly in economics in order to pave the way for his vulgar bourgeois reformism, such as "disarmament", "ultra-imperialism" and similar nonsense. The whole purpose and significance of this theoretical falsity is to obscure the *most profound* contradictions of imperialism and thus justify the theory of "unity" with the apologists of imperialism, the outright social-chauvinists and opportunists.

We have dealt at sufficient length with Kautsky's break with Marxism on this point in *Sotsial-Demokrat* and *Kommunist*. Our Russian Kautskyites, the supporters of the Organising Committee (OC),[1] headed by Akselrod and Spectator,[2] including even Martov,[3] and to a large degree Trotsky,[4] preferred to maintain a discreet silence on the question of Kautskyism, as a trend. They did not dare defend Kautsky's war-time writings, confining themselves simply to praising Kautsky (Akselrod in his German pamphlet, which the Organising Committee has *promised* to publish in Russian) or to quoting Kautsky's private letters (Spectator), in which he says he belongs to the opposition and jesuitically tries to nullify his chauvinist declarations.

It should be noted that Kautsky's "conception" of imperialism — which is tantamount to embellishing imperialism — is a retrogression not only compared with Hilferding's *Finance Capital* (no matter how assiduously Hilferding now defends Kautsky and "unity" with the social-chauvinists!) but also compared with the *social-liberal* J. A. Hobson. This English economist, who in no way claims to be a Marxist, defines imperialism, and reveals its contradictions, much more profoundly in a book published in 1902.[§] This is what Hobson (in whose book may be found nearly all Kautsky's pacifist and "conciliatory" banalities) wrote on the highly important question of the parasitic nature of imperialism:

Two sets of circumstances, in Hobson's opinion, weakened the power of the old empires: (1) "economic parasitism", and (2) formation of armies from dependent peoples. "There is first the habit of economic parasitism, by which the ruling state has

---

* "Imperialism is a product of highly developed industrial capitalism. It consists in the striving of every industrial capitalist nation to subjugate and annex ever larger *agrarian* territories, irrespective of the nations that inhabit them" (Kautsky in *Die Neue Zeit*, September 11, 1914).

used its provinces, colonies, and dependencies in order to enrich its ruling class and to bribe its lower classes into acquiescence". Concerning the second circumstance, Hobson writes:

> One of the strangest symptoms of the blindness of imperialism [this song about the "blindness" of imperialists comes more appropriately from the social-liberal Hobson than from the "Marxist" Kautsky] is the reckless indifference with which Great Britain, France, and other imperial nations are embarking on this perilous dependence. Great Britain has gone farthest. Most of the fighting by which we have won our Indian Empire has been done by natives; in India, as more recently in Egypt, great standing armies are placed under British commanders; almost all the fighting associated with our African dominions, except in the southern part, has been done for us by natives.

The prospect of partitioning China elicited from Hobson the following economic appraisal:

> The greater part of Western Europe might then assume the appearance and character already exhibited by tracts of country in the south of England, in the Riviera, and in the tourist ridden or residential parts of Italy and Switzerland, little clusters of wealthy aristocrats drawing dividends and pensions from the Far East, with a somewhat larger group of professional retainers and tradesmen and a larger body of personal servants and workers in the transport trade and in the final stages of production of the more perishable goods: all the main arterial industries would have disappeared, the staple foods and semi-manufactures flowing in as tribute from Asia and Africa …
>
> We have foreshadowed the possibility of even a larger alliance of Western states, a European federation of Great Powers which, so far from forwarding the cause of world civilisation, might introduce the gigantic peril of a Western parasitism, a group of advanced industrial nations, whose upper classes drew vast tribute from Asia and Africa, with which they supported great tame masses of retainers, no longer engaged in the staple industries of agriculture and manufacture, but kept in the performance of personal or minor industrial services under the control of a new financial aristocracy. Let those who would scout such a theory [he should have said: prospect] as undeserving of consideration examine the economic and social condition of districts in southern England today which are already reduced to this condition, and reflect upon the vast extension of such a system which might be rendered feasible by the subjection of China to the economic control of similar groups of financiers, investors [rentiers] and political and business officials, draining the greatest potential reservoir of profit the world has ever known, in order to consume it in Europe. The situation is far too complex, the play of world forces far too incalculable, to render this or any other single interpretation of

the future very probable; but the influences which govern the imperialism of Western Europe today are moving in this direction, and, unless counteracted or diverted, make towards such a consummation.

Hobson, the social-liberal, fails to see that this "counteraction" can be offered *only* by the revolutionary proletariat and *only* in the form of a social revolution. But then he is a social-liberal! Nevertheless, as early as 1902 he had an excellent insight into the meaning and significance of a "United States of Europe" (be it said for the benefit of Trotsky the Kautskyite!) and of all that is now being glossed over by the *hypocritical Kautskyites* of various countries, namely, that the *opportunists* (social-chauvinists) are working hand in glove with the imperialist bourgeoisie *precisely* towards creating an imperialist Europe on the backs of Asia and Africa, and that objectively the *opportunists* are a section of the petty bourgeoisie and of certain strata of the working class who *have been bribed* out of imperialist superprofits and converted into *watchdogs* of capitalism and *corrupters* of the labour movement.

Both in articles and in the resolutions of our Party, we have repeatedly pointed to this most profound connection, the economic connection, between the imperialist bourgeoisie and the opportunism which has triumphed (for long?) in the labour movement. And from this, incidentally, we concluded that a split with the social-chauvinists was inevitable. Our Kautskyites preferred to evade the question! Martov, for instance, uttered in his lectures a sophistry which in the *Bulletin of the Organising Committee, Secretarial Abroad* (No. 4, April 10, 1916) is expressed as follows:

> The cause of revolutionary Social-Democracy would be in a sad, indeed hopeless, plight if those groups of workers who in mental development approach most closely to the "intelligentsia" and who are the most highly skilled fatally drifted away from it towards opportunism ...

By means of the silly word "fatally" and a certain sleight-of-hand, the *fact* is *evaded* that *certain* groups of workers *have already drifted away* to opportunism and to the imperialist bourgeoisie! And that is the very fact the sophists of the OC want to *evade!* They confine themselves to the "official optimism" the Kautskyite Hilferding and many others now flaunt: objective conditions guarantee the unity of the proletariat and the victory of the revolutionary trend! We, forsooth, are "optimists" with regard to the proletariat!

But in reality all these Kautskyites — Hilferding, the OC supporters, Martov and Co. — are *optimists* ... with regard to *opportunism*. That is the whole point!

The proletariat is the child of capitalism — of world capitalism, and not only of European capitalism, or of imperialist capitalism. On a world scale, 50 years sooner or 50 years later — measured on a *world* scale this is a minor point — the "proletariat" of course "will be" united, and revolutionary Social-Democracy will "inevitably" be victorious within it. But that is not the point, Messrs. Kautskyites. The point is that at the present time, in the imperialist countries of Europe, *you are fawning* on the opportunists, who are *alien* to the proletariat as a class, who are the servants, the agents of the bourgeoisie and the vehicles of its influence, and *unless* the labour movement *rids* itself of them, it will remain a *bourgeois labour movement*. By advocating "unity" with the opportunists, with the Legiens and Davids,[5] the Plekhanovs,[6] the Chkhenkelis[7] and Potresovs,[8] etc., you are, objectively, defending the *enslavement* of the workers by the imperialist bourgeoisie with the aid of its best agents in the labour movement. The victory of revolutionary Social-Democracy on a world scale is absolutely inevitable, only it is moving and will move, is proceeding and will proceed, *against* you, it will be a victory *over* you.

These two trends, one might even say *two* parties, in the present-day labour movement, which in 1914-16 so obviously parted ways all over the world, were *traced by Engels and Marx in England* throughout the course of *decades*, roughly from 1858 to 1892.

Neither Marx nor Engels lived to see the imperialist epoch of world capitalism, which began not earlier than 1898-1900. But it has been a peculiar feature of England that even in the middle of the 19th century she already revealed at least *two* major distinguishing features of imperialism: (1) vast colonies, and (2) monopoly profit (due to her monopoly position in the world market). In both respects England at that time was an exception among capitalist countries, and Engels and Marx, analysing this exception, quite clearly and definitely indicated its *connection* with the (temporary) victory of opportunism in the English labour movement.

In a letter to Marx, dated October 7, 1858, Engels wrote:

> ... the English proletariat is actually becoming more and more bourgeois, so that this most bourgeois of all nations is apparently aiming ultimately at the possession of a bourgeois aristocracy and a bourgeois proletariat *alongside* the bourgeoisie. For a nation which exploits the whole world this is of course to a certain extent justifiable.

In a letter to Sorge,[9] dated September 21, 1872, Engels informs him that Hales[10] kicked up a big row in the Federal Council of the International and secured a vote of censure on Marx for saying that "the English labour leaders had sold themselves". Marx wrote to Sorge on August 4, 1874: "As to the urban workers here [in England], it is a pity that the whole pack of leaders did not get into Parliament. This would be the surest way of getting rid of the whole lot." In a letter to Marx, dated August

11, 1881, Engels speaks about "those very worst English trade unions which allow themselves to be led by men sold to, or at least paid by, the bourgeoisie". In a letter to Kautsky, dated September 12, 1882, Engels wrote:

> You ask me what the English workers think about. colonial policy. Well, exactly the same as they think about politics in general. There is no workers' party here, there are only Conservatives and Liberal-Radicals, and the workers gaily share the feast of England's monopoly of the world market and the colonies.

On December 7, 1889, Engels wrote to Sorge:

> The most repulsive thing here (in England) is the bourgeois ‚respectability', which has grown deep into the bones of the workers … Even Tom Mann,[11] whom I regard as the best of the lot, is fond of mentioning that he will be lunching with the Lord Mayor. If one compares this with the French, one realises what a revolution is good for, after all.

In a letter, dated April 19, 1890:

> But *under* the surface the movement [of the working class in England] is going on, is embracing ever wider sections and mostly just among the hitherto stagnant *lowest* [Engels's italics] strata. The day is no longer far off when this mass *will* suddenly *find itself*, when it will dawn upon it that it itself is this colossal mass in motion.

On March 4, 1891: "The failure of the collapsed Dockers' Union; the 'old' conservative trade unions, *rich* and therefore cowardly, remain lone on the field …" September 14, 1891: at the Newcastle Trade Union Congress the old unionists, opponents of the eight-hour day, were defeated "and the bourgeois papers recognise the defeat of the *bourgeois labour party*" (Engels's italics throughout) …

That these ideas, which were repeated by Engels over the course of decades, were also expressed by him publicly, in the press, is proved by his preface to the second edition of *The Condition of the Working Class in England,* 1892. Here he speaks of an "aristocracy among the working class", of a "privileged minority of the workers", in contradistinction to the "great mass of working people". "A small, privileged, protected minority" of the working class alone was "permanently benefited" by the privileged position of England in 1848-68, whereas "the great bulk of them experienced at best but a temporary improvement" … "With the break-down of that [England's industrial] monopoly, the English working class will lose that privileged position …" The members of the "new" unions, the unions of the unskilled workers, "had this immense advantage, that their minds were virgin soil, entirely free from the inherited 'respectable' bourgeois prejudices which hampered the brains of the better situated 'old unionists'" … "The so-called workers' representatives" in England are people "who are forgiven their being members of the working class because they themselves would like to drown their quality of being workers in the ocean of their liberalism".

We have deliberately quoted the direct statements of Marx and Engels at rather great length in order that the reader may study them *as a whole*. And they should be studied, they are worth carefully pondering over. For they are the *pivot* of the tactics in the labour movement that are dictated by the objective conditions of the imperialist era.

Here, too, Kautsky has tried to "befog the issue" and substitute for Marxism sentimental conciliation with the opportunists. Arguing against the avowed and naive social-imperialists (men like Lensch)[12] who justify Germany's participation in the war as a means of destroying England's monopoly, Kautsky "*corrects*" this obvious falsehood by another equally obvious falsehood. Instead of a cynical falsehood he employs a suave falsehood! The *industrial* monopoly of England, he says, has long ago been broken, has long ago been destroyed, and there is nothing left to destroy.

Why is this argument false?

Because, firstly, it overlooks England's *colonial* monopoly. Yet Engels, as we have seen, pointed to this very clearly as early as 1882, 34 years ago! Although England's industrial monopoly may have been destroyed, her colonial monopoly not only remains, but has become extremely accentuated, for the whole world is already divided up! By means of this suave lie Kautsky smuggles in the bourgeois-pacifist and opportunist-philistine idea that "there is nothing to fight about". On the contrary not only have the *capitalists* something to fight about now, but they *cannot help* fighting if they want to preserve capitalism, for without a forcible redivision of colonies the *new* imperialist countries cannot obtain the privileges enjoyed by the older (*and weaker*) imperialist powers.

Secondly, why does England's monopoly explain the (temporary) victory of opportunism in England? Because monopoly yields *superprofits*, i.e., a surplus of profits over and above the capitalist profits that are normal and customary all over the world. The capitalists *can* devote a part (and not a small one, at that!) of these superprofits to bribe *their own* workers, to create something like an alliance (recall the celebrated "alliances" described by the Webbs[13] of English trade unions and employers) between the workers of the given nation and their capitalists *against* the other countries. England's industrial monopoly was already destroyed by the end of the 19th century. That is beyond dispute. But *how* did this destruction take place? Did *all* monopoly disappear?

If that were so, Kautsky's "theory" of conciliation (with the opportunists) would to a certain extent be justified. But it is *not* so, and that is just the point. Imperialism *is* monopoly capitalism. Every cartel, trust, syndicate, every giant bank *is* a monopoly. Superprofits have not disappeared; they still remain. The exploitation of *all* other countries by one privileged, financially wealthy country remains and has become more intense. A handful of wealthy countries — there are only four of them, if we mean independent, really gigantic, "modern" wealth: England, France, the United States and Germany — have developed monopoly to vast proportions, they obtain *super*profits running into hundreds, if not thousands, of millions, they "ride on the backs" of hundreds and hundreds of millions of people in other countries and fight among themselves for the division of the particularly rich, particularly fat and particularly easy spoils.

This, in fact, is the economic and political essence of imperialism, the profound contradictions of which Kautsky glosses over instead of exposing.

The bourgeoisie of an imperialist "Great" Power *can economically* bribe the upper strata of "its" workers by spending on this a hundred million or so francs a year, for its *super*profits most likely amount to about a thousand million. And how this little sop is divided among the labour ministers, "labour representatives" (remember Engels's splendid analysis of the term), labour members of war industries committees, labour officials, workers belonging to the narrow craft unions, office employees, etc., etc., is a secondary question.

Between 1848 and 1868, and to a certain extent even later, only England enjoyed a monopoly: *that is why* opportunism could prevail there for decades. *No* other countries possessed either very rich colonies or an industrial monopoly.

The last third of the 19th century saw the transition to the new, imperialist era. Finance capital *not* of one, but of several, though very few, Great Powers enjoys a monopoly. (In Japan and Russia the monopoly of military power, vast territories, or special facilities for robbing minority nationalities, China, etc., partly supplements, partly takes the place of, the monopoly of modern, up-to-date finance capital.) This difference explains why England's monopoly position *could* remain *unchallenged* for decades. The monopoly of modern finance capital is being frantically challenged; the era of imperialist wars has begun. It was possible in those days to bribe and corrupt the working class of *one* country for decades. This is now improbable, if not impossible. But on the other hand, *every* imperialist "Great" Power can and does bribe *smaller* strata (than in England in 1848-68) of the "labour aristocracy". Formerly a "*bourgeois labour party*", to use Engels's remarkably profound expression, could arise only in one country, because it alone enjoyed a monopoly, but, on the other hand, it could exist for a long time. Now a *"bourgeois labour party" is inevitable* and typical in *all* imperialist countries; but in view of the desperate struggle they are waging for the division of spoils, it is improbable that such a party can prevail for long in a number of countries. For the trusts, the financial oligarchy, high prices, etc., while *enabling* the bribery of a handful in the top layers, are increasingly oppressing, crushing, ruining and torturing the *mass* of the proletariat and the semi-proletariat.

On the one hand, there is the tendency of the bourgeoisie and the opportunists to convert a handful of very rich and privileged nations into "eternal" parasites on the body of the rest of mankind, to "rest on the laurels" of the exploitation of Negroes, Indians, etc., keeping them in subjection with the aid of the excellent weapons of extermination provided by modern militarism. On the other hand, there is the tendency of the *masses*, who are more oppressed than before and who bear the whole brunt of imperialist wars, to cast off this yoke and to overthrow the bourgeoisie. It is in the struggle between these two tendencies that the history of the labour movement will now inevitably develop. For the first tendency is not accidental; it is "substantiated" economically. In *all* countries the bourgeoisie has already begotten, fostered and secured for itself "bourgeois labour parties" of social-chauvinists. The difference between a definitely formed party, like Bissolati's in Italy, for example, which is fully social-imperialist, and, say, the semi-formed near-party of the Potresovs, Gvozdyovs,[14] Bulkins,[15] Chkheidzes,[16] Skobelevs[17] and Co., is an immaterial difference. The important thing is that, economically, the desertion of a stratum of the labour aristocracy to the bourgeoisie has matured and become an accomplished fact; and this economic fact, this shift in class relations, will find political form, in one shape or another, without any particular "difficulty".

On the economic basis referred to above, the political institutions of modern capitalism — press, parliament, associations, congresses, etc. — have created *political* privileges and sops for the respectful, meek, reformist and patriotic office employees and workers, corresponding to the economic privileges and sops. Lucrative and soft jobs in the government or on the war industries committees, in parliament and on diverse committees, on the editorial staffs of "respectable", legally published newspapers or on the management councils of no less respectable and "bourgeois law-abiding" trade unions — this is the bait by which the imperialist bourgeoisie attracts and rewards the representatives and supporters of the "bourgeois labour parties".

The mechanics of political democracy works in the same direction. Nothing in our times can be done without elections; nothing can be done without the masses. And in this era of printing and parliamentarism it is *impossible* to gain the following of the masses without a widely ramified, systematically managed, well-equipped system of flattery, lies, fraud, juggling with fashionable and popular catchwords, and promising all manner of reforms and blessings to the workers right and left — as long as they renounce the revolutionary struggle for the overthrow of the bourgeoisie. I would call this system Lloyd-Georgism, after the English Minister Lloyd George,[18] one of the foremost and most dexterous representatives of this system in the classic land of the "bourgeois labour party". A first-class bourgeois manipulator, an astute politician, a popular orator who will deliver any speeches you like, even r-r-revolutionary ones, to a labour audience, and a man who is capable of obtaining sizable sops for docile workers in the shape of social reforms (insurance, etc.), Lloyd George serves the bourgeoisie splendidly,* and serves it precisely *among* the workers, brings its influence *precisely* to the proletariat, to where the bourgeoisie needs it most and where it finds it most difficult to subject the masses morally.

And is there such a great difference between Lloyd George and the Scheidemanns, Legiens, Hendersons[19] and Hyndmans, Plekhanovs, Renaudels[20] and Co.? Of the latter, it may be objected, some will return to the revolutionary socialism of Marx. This is possible, but it is an insignificant difference in degree, if the question is regarded from its political, i.e., its mass aspect. Certain individuals among the present social-chauvinist leaders may return to the proletariat. But the social-chauvinist or (what is the same thing) opportunist *trend* can neither disappear nor "return" to the revolutionary proletariat. Wherever Marxism is popular among the workers, this political trend, this "bourgeois labour party", will swear by the name of Marx. It cannot be prohibited from doing this, just as a trading firm cannot be prohibited from using any particular label, sign or advertisement. It has always been the case in history that after the death of revolutionary leaders who were popular among the oppressed classes, their enemies have attempted to appropriate their names so as to deceive the oppressed classes.

The fact is that "bourgeois labour parties", as a political phenomenon, have already been formed in *all* the foremost capitalist countries, and that unless a determined and relentless struggle is waged all along the line against these parties — or groups, trends, etc., it is all the same — there can be no question of a struggle against imperialism, or of Marxism, or of a socialist labour movement. The Chkheidze faction, *Nashe Dyelo*[20] and *Golos Truda*[21] in Russia, and the OC supporters abroad are nothing but

---

* I recently read an article in an English magazine by a Tory, a political opponent of Lloyd George, entitled "Lloyd George from the standpoint of a Tory". The war opened the eyes of this opponent and made him realise what an excellent servant of the bourgeoisie this Lloyd George is! The Tories have made peace with him!

varieties of one *such* party. There is not the slightest reason for thinking that these parties will disappear *before* the social revolution. On the contrary, the nearer the revolution approaches, the more strongly it flares up and the more sudden and violent the transitions and leaps in its progress, the greater will be the part the struggle of the revolutionary mass stream against the opportunist petty-bourgeois stream will play in the labour movement. Kautskyisin is not an independent trend, because it has no roots either in the masses or in the privileged stratum which has deserted to the bourgeoisie. But the danger of Kautskyism lies in the fact that, utilising the ideology of the past, it endeavours to reconcile the proletariat with the "bourgeois labour party", to preserve the unity of the proletariat with that party and thereby enhance the latter's prestige. The masses no longer follow the avowed social-chauvinists: Lloyd George has been hissed down at workers' meetings in England; Hyndman has left the party; the Renaudels and Scheidemanns, the Potresovs and Gvozdyovs are protected by the police. The Kautskyites' masked defence of the social-chauvinists is much more dangerous.

One of the most common sophistries of Kautskyism is its reference to the "masses". We do not want, they say, to break away from the masses and mass organisations! But just think how Engels put the question. In the 19th century the "mass organisations" of the English trade unions were on the side of the bourgeois labour party. Marx and Engels did not reconcile themselves to it on this ground; they exposed it. They did not forget, firstly, that the trade union organisations directly embraced a *minority of the proletariat*. In England then, as in Germany now, not more than one-fifth of the proletariat was organised. No one can seriously think it possible to organise the majority of the proletariat under capitalism. Secondly — and this is the main point — it is not so much a question of the size of an organisation, as of the real, objective significance of its policy: does its policy represent the masses, does it serve them, i.e., does it aim at their liberation from capitalism, or does it represent the interests of the minority, the minority's reconciliation with capitalism? The latter was true of England in the 19th century, and it is true of Germany, etc., now.

Engels draws a distinction between the "bourgeois labour party" of the *old* trade unions — the privileged minority — and the "*lowest* mass", the real majority, and appeals to the latter, who are *not* infected by "bourgeois respectability". This is the essence of Marxist tactics!

Neither we nor anyone else can calculate precisely what portion of the proletariat is following and will follow the social-chauvinists and opportunists. This will be revealed only by the struggle, it will be definitely decided only by the socialist revolution.

But we know for certain that the "defenders of the fatherland" in the imperialist war *represent* only a minority. And it is therefore our duty, if we wish to remain socialists, to go down *lower* and *deeper*, to the real masses; this is the whole meaning and the whole purport of the struggle against opportunism. By exposing the fact that the opportunists and social-chauvinists are in reality betraying and selling the interests of the masses, that they are defending the temporary privileges of a minority of the workers, that they are the vehicles of bourgeois ideas and influences, that they are really allies and agents of the bourgeoisie, we teach the masses to appreciate their true political interests, to fight for socialism and for the revolution through all the long and painful vicissitudes of imperialist wars and imperialist armistices.

The only Marxist line in the world labour movement is to explain to the masses the inevitability and necessity of breaking with opportunism, to educate them for revolution by waging a relentless struggle against opportunism, to utilise the experiences of the war to expose, not conceal, the utter vileness of national-liberal labour politics. +

* * * * *

NOTES

The following notes have been provided by the editors with the exception of the notes to the main text of "Imperialism", which are by Lenin.

INTRODUCTION

1   V.I. Lenin, *Collected Works* (Progress Publishers: Moscow 1977), Vol. 37, p. 365

2   Lenin listed the "shortcomings" of Hilferding's analysis of imperialism in his notebooks as "(1) Theoretical error concerning money. (2) Ignores (almost) the division of the world. (3) Ignores the relationship between finance capital and parasitism. (4) Ignores the relationship between imperialism and opportunism" (V.I. Lenin, *Collected Works*, Vol. 39, p. 202).

3   *ibid.*, pp. 264-65

4   *ibid.*, p. 266

5   Cited in W.A. Williams, *The Tragedy of American Diplomacy* (Delta: New York, 1962), p. 66.

6   *ibid.*, pp. 78-79

7   V.I. Lenin, Introduction to N. Bukharin, *Imperialism and World Economy* (Merlin Press: London 1972), pp. 10-11. The chief weakness of Bukharin's analysis of

imperialism was that it defined it as "the policy of conquest of finance capital" (*ibid.*, p. 115).

8   K. Marx and F. Engels, *Selected Works* (Progress Publishers: Moscow 1977), Vol. 1, pp. 503-04

9   K. Marx, *Capital*, Vol. 3 (Penguin Books: Harmondsworth 1981), pp. 567-69

10   *ibid.*, pp. 1045-46

11   See below, pp. 100, 120.

12   K. Marx and F. Engels, *Selected Works*, Vol. 1, p. 504

13   K. Marx and F. Engels, *The Communist Manifesto and Its Relevance for Today* (Resistance Books: Sydney, 1998), p. 46

14   K. Marx and F. Engels, *Selected Works*, Vol. 3, p. 450

15   *ibid.*, p. 447

16   *ibid.*, p. 448

17   *ibid.*, p. 447

18   V.I. Lenin, *Collected Works*, Vol. 31, p. 230

PREFACE TO THE FRENCH AND GERMAN EDITIONS

1   The *Treaty of Brest-Litovsk* was signed in the Belorussian town of Brest-Litovsk (Brest) on March 3, 1918 by representatives of Soviet Russia on the one side and those of Imperial Germany, the Austro-Hungarian Empire, Bulgaria and Turkey on the other. It brought an end to Russia's participation in the first world war.

2   The *Treaty of Versailles* concluded World War I (1914-18) and was signed on June 28, 1919 by representatives of the Allied Powers (Britain, France, Italy, Japan and the USA), on the one hand, and Germany, on the other. The treaty imposed harsh reparation conditions upon Germany.

3   *Wilsonism* refers to the policies of Woodrow Wilson, president of the United States from 1913 to 1921, in particular, his camouflaging of US imperialist objectives in entering World War I with demagogic rhetoric about "democracy" and "the self-determination of nations".

4   Eduard *Bernstein* (1850-1929) was a leading figure in the German Social-Democratic Party (SPD) who, from the late 1890s on, advocated a reformist "revision" of Marxism. Alexander *Millerand* (1859-1943) was a French socialist parliamentarian who in 1899 became a minister in the French bourgeois government. Henry *Hyndman* (1842-1921) was the founder of the British Social-Democratic Federation in 1881 and of the British Socialist Party in 1911. He led a pro-war split from the SP in 1916, called the National

Socialist Party. Samuel *Gompers* (1850-1924) was the president of the craft-union-based American Federation of Labor from 1886 to 1924, an outspoken supporter of class-collaboration and US imperialist foreign policy.

5 The *Independent Social-Democratic Party of Germany* (USPD) was formed in April 1917 as a pacifist breakaway from the pro-war SPD. Among its leaders were Eduard Bernstein and Karl Kautsky. At its founding it had 120,000 members. It participated in the bourgeois-republican provisional government headed by SPD leader Freidrich Ebert in November-December 1918. It attained a maximum membership of 750,000 by November 1919. In 1920 the USPD majority fused with the Communist Party of Germany (KPD), while the minority retained the party name until rejoining the SPD in 1922.

6 *Kolchak and Denikin* were former tsarist military officers who commanded counterrevolutionary White armies during the 1918-20 Russian Civil War. Admiral A.V. Kolchak (1873-1920) headed the White armies in Siberia. General A.I. Denekin (1872-1947) comanded the White armies in southern Russia.

7 The *Mensheviks* originated as an opportunist minority faction of the Russian Social-Democratic Labour Party at its 2nd congress in 1903. In 1912 the Bolshevik faction led by Lenin expelled the Mensheviks from the RSDLP. They supported and participated in the bourgeois Provisional Government in 1917. During the civil war that followed the Bolshevik-led overthrow of the Provisional Government by the soviets (councils) of workers', soldiers' and peasants' deputies in November 1917, one wing of the Mensheviks supported the counterrevolutionary White armies.

8 The *Socialist-Revolutionaries* originated as a party in 1901-02 in opposition to the Marxist RSDLP. They espoused a petty-bourgeois democratic program of "land socialisation" (abolition of herediary landlordism and division of the landlord estates among the peasant masses) as the basis of an agrarian-based "socialism". During 1917 their leaders supported and participated in the Provisional Government. Toward the end of 1917 the SR Party split into pro- and anti-Bolshevik wings. The Left SRs supported the October Revolution and participated in the Soviet government until July 1918 when they organised an attempted coup against the Bolsheviks. During the Russian Civil War both wings of the SRs aligned themselves with the monarchist-led White armies against the Soviet workers' and peasants' republic.

9 Philipp *Scheidemann* (1865-1939) and Gustav *Noske* (1868-1946) were leading members of the Social-Democratic Party of Germany (SPD), and ministers in the SPD-led provisional government that suppressed the revolutionary workers' movement in Germany in 1918-19.

10 The *Spartacists* originated as a revolutionary current in the German Social-Democratic

Party (SPD) during World War I, opposing the SPD leadership's pro-war position. *Spartacus* was the name of the newsletter issued by the Internationale Group set up in January 1916. On November 11, 1918 the group constituted itself as an independent organisation, the Spartacus League, operating as public faction within the Independent Social-Democratic Party of Germany (USPD). On January 1, 1919 the Berlin-based Spartacus League fused with other revolutionary groups in Germany to form the Communist Party (KPD). In January 1919 the best known leaders of the Spartacists, Rosa Luxemburg and Karl Liebkneckt, were arrested and murdered by the SPD-led provisional government.

11 The *Versaillais* were the supporters of the bourgeois-republican government set up in Versailles after the popular overthrow of bourgeois rule in Paris in March 1870 and the establishment of the revolutionary Paris Commune. The *"Communards"* were the supporters of the revolutionary democracy established in Paris from March 18 to May 22, 1870. Following its military victory over the Commune, the Versaillais army massacred between 20,000 and 30,000 Communards.

LENIN'S NOTES TO 'IMPERIALISM'

1   Figures taken from *Annalen des deutschen Reichs*, 1911, Zahn.

2   *Statistical Abstract of the United States 1912*, p. 202

3   *Finance Capital*, Russ. ed., pp. 286-87

4   Hans Gideon Heymann, *Die gemischten Werke im deutschen Grosseisengewerbe* [Combined Plants in the German Big Iron Industry], Stuttgart, 1904, (S. 256, 278)

5   Hermann Levy, *Monopole, Kartelle und Trusts*, Jena, 1909, S. 286, 290, 298

6   Th. Vogelstein, "Die finanzielle Organisation der kapitalistischen Industrie und die Monopolbildungen" [Financial Organisation of the Capitalist Industry and the Formation of Monopolies] in *Grundriss der Sozialökonomik* [Outline of Social Economics], VI Abt., Tübingen, 1914. Cf., also by the same author: *Organisationsformen der Eisenindustrie und Textilindustrie in England und Amerika* [The Organisational Forms of the Iron and Textile Industry of England and America], Bd. I, Lpz., 1910.

7   Dr. Riesser, *Die deutschen Grossbanken und ihre Konzentration im Zusammenhange mit der Entwicklung der Gesamtwirtschaft in Deutschland* [The German Big Banks and Their Concentration in Connection with the Development of the General Economy in Germany], 4. Aufl., 1912, S. 149; Robert Liefmann, *Kartelle und Trusts und die Weiterbildung der volkswirtschaftlichen Organisation* [Cartels and Trusts and the Further Development of Economic Organisation], 2. Aufl., 1910, S. 25

8   Dr. Fritz Kestner, *Der Organisationstwang. Eine Untersuchung über die Kampfe*

zwischen Kartellen und Aussenseitern [Compulsory Organisation An Investigation of the Struggle Between Cartels and Outsiders], Berlin, 1912, S. 11.

9   R. Liefmann, *Beteiligungs- und Finanzierungsgesellschaften. Eine Studie über den modernen Kapitalismus und das Eflektenwesen* [Holding and Finance Companies. A Study in Modern Capitalism and Securities], I. Aufl., Jena, 1909, S. 212

10 Ibid., S. 218

11 Dr. S. Tschierschky, *Kartell und Trust*, Göttingen, 1903, S. 13

12 Th. Vogelstein, *Organisationsformen*, S. 275

13 *Report of the Commissioner of Corporations on the Tobacco Industry*, Washington, 1909, p. 266, cited according to Dr. Paul Tafel, *Die nordamerikanischen Trusts und ihre Wirkungen auf den Fortschritt der Technik* [North American Trusts and Their Effect on Technical Progress], Stuttgart, 1913, S. 48

14 Dr. P. Tafel, ibid., S. 49

15 Riesser, op. cit., third edition, p. 547 et seq. The newspapers (June 1916) report the formation of a new gigantic trust which combines the chemical industry of Germany.

16 Kestner, op. cit., S. 254

17 L. Eschwege, "Zement" in *Die Bank*, 1909, 1, S. 15 et seq

18 Jeidels, *Das Verhältnis der deutschen Grossbanken zur Industrie mit besonderer Berucksichtigung der Eisenindustrie* [The Relationship of the German Big Banks to Industry, With Special Reference to the Iron Industry], Leipzig, 1905, S. 271

19 Liefmann, *Beteiligungs- und Finanzierungsgesellschaften*, S. 434

20 Ibid., S. 465-66

21 Jeidels, op. cit., S. 108

22 Alfred Lansburgh, "Funf Jahre deutsches Bankwesen" [Five Years of German Banking], in *Die Bank*, 1913, No. 8, S. 728

23 Schulze-Gaevernitz, "Die deutsche Kreditbank" in *Grundriss der Sozialökonomik* [The German Credit Bank in Outline of Social Economics], Tübingen, 1915, S. 12 and 137

24 R. Liefmann, *Beteiligungs- und Finanzierungsgesellschaften. Eine Studie über den modernen Kapitalismus und das Effektenwesen*, 1 Aufl., Jena, 1909, S. 212

25 Alfred Lansburgh, "Das Beteiligungssystem im deutschen Bankwesen" [The Holding System in German Banking] in *Die Bank*, 1910, 1, S.500

26 Eugen Kaufmann, *Das französische Bankwesen*, Tübingen, 1911, S. 356 und 362

27 Jean Lescure, *L'épargne en France* [Savings in France], Paris, 1914, p. 52

28 A. Lansburgh, "Die Bank mit den 300 Millionen" in *Die Bank*, 1914, 1, S. 426

29 S. Tschierschky, op.cit., S.128

30 *Statistics of the National Monetary Commission*, quoted in *Die Bank*, 1910, 1, S.1200

31 *Die Bank*, 1913, S. 811, 1022; 1914, S. 713

32 *Die Bank*, 1914, S. 316

33 Dr. Oscar Stillich, *Geld- und Bankwesen*, Berlin, 1907, S. 169

34 Schulze-Gaevernitz, "Die deutsche Kreditbank" in *Grundriss der Sozialökonomik*, Tübingen, 1915, S. 101

35 Riesser, op. cit., 4th ed, S. 629

36 Schulze-Gaevernitz, "Die deutsche Kreditbank" in *Grundriss der Socialökonomik*, Tübingen, 1915, S. 151

37 *Die Bank*, 1912, 1, S. 435

38 Quoted by Schulze-Gaevernitz, op. cit., S. 155

39 Jeidels, op. cit.; Riesser, op. cit

40 Jeidels, op. cit., S. 157

41 An article by Eug. Kaufmann on French banks in *Die Bank*, 1909, 2, S. 851 et seq.

42 Dr. Oscar Stillich, *Geld und Bankwesen*, Berlin, 1907, S. 148

43 Jeidels, op. cit., S. 183-84

44 Ibid., S. 181

45 R. Hilferding, *Finance Capital*, Moscow, 1912 (in Russian), pp. 338-39

46 R. Liefmann, op. cit., S. 476

47 Hans Gideon Heymann, *Die gemischten Werke im deutschen Grosseisengewerbe*, Stuttgart, 1904, S. 268-69

48 Liefmann, *Beteiligungsgesellschaften*, etc., S. 258 of the first edition

49 Schulze-Gaevernitz in *Grundriss da Sozialökonomie*, V, 2, S. 110

50 L. Eschwege, "Tochtergesellschaften" [Subsidiary Companies] in *Die Bank*, 1914, 1, S.545

51 Kurt Heinig, "Der Weg des Elektrotrusts" [The Path of the Electric Trust] in *Die Neue Zeit*, 1912, 30. Jahrg., 2, S. 484

52 E. Agahd, *Grossbanken und Weltmark. Die wirtschaftliche und politische Bedeutung der Grossbanken im Weltmarkt unter Berücksichtigung ihres Einflusses auf Russlands Volkswirtschaft und die deutschrussischen Beziehungen* [Big Banks and the World Market. The economic and political significance of the big banks on the world market, with reference to their influence on Russia's national economy and German-Russian relations], Berlin, 1914.

53 Lysis, *Contre l'oligarchie financière en France* [Against the Financial Oligarchy in

France], 5 éd., Paris, 1908, pp. 11, 12, 26, 39, 40, 48

54 *Die Bank*, 1913, No. 7, S. 630

55 Stillich, op. cit., S. 143, also W. Sombart, *Die deutsche Volkswirtschaft im 19. Jahrhundert* [German National Economy in the 19th Century], 2. Aufl., 1909, S. 526, Anlage 8

56 *Finance Capital*, p. 172

57 Stillich, op. cit., S. 138, and Liefmann, S. 51

58 In *Die Bank*, 1913, S. 952, L, Eschwege, *Der Sumpf*; ibid., 1912, 1, S. 223 et seq

59 "Verkehrstrust" in *Die Bank*, 1914, I, S. 89

60 "Der Zug zur Bank" [The Attraction of the Bank] in *Die Bank*, 1909, 1, S. 79

61 Ibid., S. 301

62 Ibid., 1911, 2, S. 825; 1913, 2, S. 962

63 E. Agahd, op. cit., S. 202

64 *Bulletin de l'institut international da statistique*, t. XIX, livr. II, La Haye, 1912. Data concerning small states, second column, are estimated by adding 20% to the 1902 figures.

65 Hobson. *Imperialism*, London, 1902, p. 58; Riesser, op. cit., S. 395 und 404; P. Arndt in *Weltwirtschaftliches Archiv*, Bd. 7, 1916, S. 35, Neymarck in *Bulletin*; Hilferding, *Finance Capital*, p. 492; Lloyd George, Speech in the House of Commons, May 4, 1915, reported in the *Daily Telegraph*, May 5, 1915; B. Harms, *Probleme der Weltwirtschaft*, Jena, 1912, S. 235 et seq.; Dr. Siegmund Schilder, *Entwicklungstendenzen der Weltwirtschaft* [Trends of Development of World Economy], Berlin, 1912, Band I, S. 150; George Paish, "Great Britain's Capital Investments, etc.," in *Journal of the Royal Statistical Society*, Vol. LXXIV, 1910-11, p. 167 et seq.; Georges Diouritch, *L'Expansion des banques allemandes a l'étranger, ses rapports avec le développement économique de l'Allemagne* [Expansion of German Banks Abroad in Connection with the Economic Development of Germany], Paris, 1909, p. 84

66 *Die Bank*, 1913, 2, S. 1024

67 Schilder, op. cit., S. 346, 350 and 371

68 Riesser, op. cit., 4th ed., S. 375; Diouritch, p. 283

69 *The Annals of the American Academy of Political and Social Science*, Vol. LIX, May 1915, p. 301. In the same volume on p. 331, we read that the well-known statistician Paish, in the last issue of the financial magazine *The Statist*, estimated the amount of capital exported by Britain, Germany, France, Belgium and Holland at $40,000 million, i.e., 200,000 million francs.

70 Jeidels, op. cit., S. 232

71 Riesser, op. cit.; Diouritch, op. cit., p. 239; Kurt Heining, op. cit

72 Jeidels, op. cit., S. 193

73 Diouritch, op. cit., p. 245

74 *Die Bank*, 1912, 1, S. 1036; 1912, 2, S. 629; 1913, 1, S. 388

75 Riesser, op. cit., S. 125

76 Vogelstein, *Organisationsformen*, S. 100

77 Liefmann, *Kartelle und Trusts*, 2. A., S. 161

78 A. Supan, *Die territoriale Entwicklung der europäischen Kolonien*, 1906, S. 254

79 Henry C. Morris, *The History of Colonisation*, New York, 1900, Vol. II, p. 88; Vol. I, p. 419; Vol. II, p. 304

80 *Die Neue Zeit*, XVI, I, 1898, S. 302

81 Ibid., S. 304

82 C. P. Lucas, *Greater Rome and Greater Britain*, Oxford, 1912 or the Earl of Cromer's *Ancient and Modern Imperialism*, London, 1910.

83 Schilder, op. cit., S. 38-42

84 Wahl, *La France aux colonies* [France in the Colonies], quoted by Henri Russier, *Le partage de l'Océanie* [The Partition of Oceania], Paris, 1905, p. 165

85 Schulze-Gaevernitz, *Britischer Imperialismus und engliseber Freihandel zu Beginn des 20-ten Jabrhunderts* [British Imperialism and English Free Trade at the Beginning of the 20th Century], Leipzig, 1906, S. 318. Sartorius v. Waltershausen says the same in *Das volkswirtschaftiche System der Kapitalanlage im Auslande* [The National Economic System of Capital Investments Abroad], Berlin, 1907, S. 46

86 Schilder, op. cit., Vol. 1, S. 160-61

87 J. I. Driault, *Problémes politiques et sociaux*, Paris, 1907 p. 299

88 *Die Neue Zeit*, 1914, 2 (B. 32), S. 909, Sept. 11, 1914; cf. 1915, 2, S. 107 et seq

89 Hobson, *Imperialism*, London, 1902, p. 324

90 *Die Neue Zeit*, 1914, 2 (B. 32), S. 921, Sept. 11, 1914. Cf. 1915, 2, S. 107 et seq

91 *Die Neue Zeit*, 1915 1, S. 144, April 30. 1915

92 R. Calwer, *Einführung in die Weltwirtschaft*, Berlin, 1906

93 *Statistisches Jahrbuch für das deutsche Reich, 1915*; *Archiv für Eisenbahnwesen*, 1892 [Statistical Yearbook for the German Empire; Railroad Archive]. Minor details for the distribution of railways among the colonies of the various countries in 1890 had to be estimated approximately.

94 Cf. also Edgar Crammond, "The Economic Relations of the British and German Em-

pires" in *The Journal of the Royal Statistical Society*, July 1914, p.777 et seq

95   Hobson, op. cit., pp. 59, 60

96   Schulze-Gaevernitz, *Britischer Imperialismus*, S.320 et seq

97   Sartorius von Waltershausen, *Das volkswirtschaftliche System, etc.*, Berlin, 1907, Buch IV

98   Schilder, op. cit., S. 393

99   Schulze-Gaevernitz, op. cit, S. 122

100 *Die Bank*, 1911, 1, S. 10-11

101 Hobson, op. cit., pp. 103, 205, 144, 335, 186

102 Gerhard Hildebrand, *Die Erschütterung der Industrieherrschaft und des Industriesozialismus* [The Shattering of the Rule of Industrialism and Industrial Socialism], 1910, S. 229 et seq

103 Schulze-Gaevernitz, *Britischer Imperialismus*, S. 301

104 *Statistik des Deutschen Reichs*, Bd. 211

105 Henger, *Die Kapitalsanlage der Franzosen* [French Investments], Stuttgart, 1913

106 Hourwich, *Immigration and Labour*, New York, 1913.

107 Briefwechsel von Marx und Engels, Bd. II, S. 290; IV, 453 — Karl Kautsky, *Sozialismus und Kolonialpolitik*, Berlin, 1907, S. 79; this pamphlet was written by Kautsky in those infinitely distant days when he was still a Marxist.

108 Russian social-chauvinism in its overt form represented by the Potresovs, Chkhenkelis, Maslovs, etc. and in its covert form (Chkheidze, Skobelev, Axelrod, Martov, etc.), also emerged from the Russian variety of opportunism, namely, liquidationism.

109 *Weltwirtschaftliches Archiv*, Bd. II, p. 193

110 J. Patouillet, *L'impérialisme américain*, Dijon, 1904, p. 272

111 *Bulletin de l'Institut International de Statistique*, t. XIX, livr. II, p. 225

112 Kautsky, *Nationalstaat, imperialistischer Staat und Staatenbund* [National State, Imperialist State and Union of States], Nürnberg, 1915, S. 72, 70

113 *Finance Capital*, p. 567

114 *Die Bank*, 1909, 2, S. 819 et seq

115 *Die Neue Zeit*, April 30, 1915, S. 144

116 David Jayne Hill, *A History of the Diplomacy in the International Development of Europe*, Vol. 1, p. x

117 Schilder, op. cit., S. 178

118 *Finance Capital*, p.487

119 *Grundriss der Sozialökonomik*, S. 146

APPENDIX: IMPERIALISM AND THE SPLIT IN SOCIALISM

1   The *Organising Committee* (OC) was set up in August 1912 by a conference of anti-Bolshevik Russian Social-Democrats and formed the leading body of the Mensheviks in 1917, when it was replaced at the August 1917 Menshevik "Unity" congress by the Central Committee of the Russian Social-Democratic Labour Party (Mensheviks).

2   Pavel *Akselrod* (1850-1928), a leading Menshevik, was a member of the Secretariat of the Organising Committee Abroad during World War I. *Spectator* was a pseudonym used by M.I. Nakimson (1880-1938), a Russian economist and member of the pro-Menshevik Bund (the General Jewish Union of Lithuania, Poland and Russia).

3   Julius *Martov* (1973-1923) was a leader of the RSDLP and of the Mensheviks after 1903 and head of the Secretariat of the Organising Committee Abroad during World War I.

4   Leon *Trotsky* (1879-1940) was a leading member of the RSDLP. He aligned himself with the Mensheviks in 1903-04, after which he took an independent position within the RSDLP. He played a central role in organising the August 1912 conference of anti-Bolshevik Russian Social-Democrats in Vienna that set up the Organising Committee, which soon became dominated by the Mensheviks. During the first world war he took an anti-war position but opposed the Bolshevik party's policy of calling for an organisational break with the Kautskyite "Centre" current in the socialist movement. In July 1917 he joined the Bolsheviks.

5   Carl *Legion* (1861-1920) and Eduard *David* (1863-1936) were leading members of the right-wing of the Social-Democratic Party of Germany (SPD) and outspoken apologists for German imperialism during World War I. Legion was head of the German trade union movement.

6   Georgy *Plekhanov* (1856-1918) was the founder of the Russian Marxist movement. He originally sided with the Bolsheviks at the RSDLP 2nd congress in 1903, but shortly after became a Menshevik. During World War I he adopted a strong pro-war stance.

7   Akaky *Chkhenkeli* (1874-1959) was a leading Menshevik who subsequently became foreign minister of the Menshevik-led Georgian republic from 1918 to 1921.

8   Aleksandr *Potresov* (1869-1934) was an early Russian Marxist and after 1903 a leading Menshevik.

9   Friedrich *Sorge* (1828-1906) a close collaborator of Marx and Engels. Following the 1848-49 revolutionary upsurge in Germany, he emigrated to the United States. He was

secretary of the International Working Men's Association (the First International) in 1872.

10 John *Hales* (b. 1839) was a leader of the English trade union movement and secretary of the General Council of the First International from 1866 to 1872. He led the reformist wing of the British Federal Council of the International.

11 *Tom Mann* (1856-1941) was an English trade union leader. In 1885 he joined the left-wing of the British Social-Democratic Federation. In the late 1880s he played a leading role in organising unskilled workers into trade unions.

12 Paul *Lensch* (1873-1926) was a left-wing SPD member who adopted a pro-war stand during World War I.

13 The *Webbs* (Beatrice and Sydney) were writers on the history of the English labour movement and leading figures in the Fabian Society, an organisation of English social-reformists.

14 Kuzma *Gvozdyov* (b. 1883) was a leading Menshevik and chair of the workers' group in the tsarist government's Central War Industries Committee during World war I.

15 Fyodor *Bulkin* (b. 1888) was a right-wing Menshevik.

16 Nikolai *Chkheidze* (1864-1926) was a Georgian Social-Democrat and leader of the Menshevik group in the tsarist parliament (Duma). He was first president of the Petrograd Soviet in 1917.

17 Matvei *Skobolev* (1885-1939) was a Menshevik deputy in the Duma during World War I and became vice-president of the Petrograd Soviet and minister of labour in the Provisional Government in 1917.

18 David *Lloyd George* (1863-1945) was leader of the British Liberal Party and British prime minister, 1916-22.

19 Arthur *Henderson* (1863-1935) was a British trade union leader and secetary of the Labour Party from 1911 to 1932. He was a Cabinet minister during the First World War.

20 Pierre *Renaudel* (1871-1935) was a leader of the left-wing of the French Socialist Party who defected to the party's right-wing at the beginning of World War I. He was editor of the SP's daily paper, *l'Humanité* from 1914 to 1918.

21 *Nashe Dyelo (Our Cause) was a Menshevik monthly published in Petrograd (St. Petersburg) in 1915. Six issues appeared.*

22 *Golos Truda (Voice of Labour) was a legal Menshevik magazine published in Samara in 1916 after the closure of Nashe Dyelo. Three issues appeared.*

www.ingramcontent.com/pod-product-compliance
Lightning Source LLC
Chambersburg PA
CBHW050842270326
41930CB00019B/3442